# In BOD We Trust

# In BOD We Trust

## BRIAN O'DRISCOLL

### THE BIOGRAPHY OF IRELAND'S
### GREATEST RUGBY HERO

MARCUS STEAD

JOHN BLAKE

Published by John Blake Publishing Ltd,
3 Bramber Court, 2 Bramber Road,
London W14 9PB, England

www.blake.co.uk

First published in hardback in 2008

ISBN: 978-1-84454-545-2

British Library Cataloguing-in-Publication Data:

A catalogue record for this book is available from the British Library.

Design by www.envydesign.co.uk

Printed in the UK by CPI William Clowes Ltd, Beccles, NR34 7TL

1 3 5 7 9 10 8 6 4 2

Papers used by John Blake Publishing are natural, recyclable
products made from wood grown in sustainable forests.
The manufacturing processes conform to the environmental
regulations of the country of origin.

Every attempt has been made to contact the relevant copyright-holders,
but some were unobtainable. We would be grateful if the appropriate
people could contact us.

# CONTENTS

CHAPTER 1    RAPID RISE TO THE TOP      1

CHAPTER 2    COMING OF AGE      29

CHAPTER 3    THE GREATEST HONOUR,      57
                THE GREATEST CHALLENGE

CHAPTER 4    LEADING BY EXAMPLE      67

CHAPTER 5    DOWN TO BUSINESS      89

CHAPTER 6    THE CHANCE OF A LIFETIME      115

CHAPTER 7    MOVING ON      135

CHAPTER 8    BACK IN BUSINESS      157

CHAPTER 9    LEADING LEINSTER      183

CHAPTER 10   A DATE WITH DESTINY      217

CHAPTER 11   THROWING IT ALL AWAY      241

# CHAPTER 1

# RAPID RISE TO THE TOP

Brian O'Driscoll was born on 21 January 1979 with rugby in his blood. He weighed in at 9lb 12oz and cried, it seemed, for months without stopping. It later transpired that this was due to hunger. Little did his parents know that he would actually turn out to be a shy and very quiet child.

His father, Frank, was a decent centre in his day, who has been described by his son as a mad kamikaze tackler with a good step and plenty of wheels. He had toured Argentina with Ireland in the 1970s and played in the 'Tests', but in those days caps weren't awarded for matches against the Pumas.

He was unlucky in some ways. With the great Mike

Gibson around, he did not get to fulfil his ambition to play for his country more often; much later on he would get enormous pleasure from living his dreams through his son, who would become more of a friend than a son as the years progressed.

Brian's early years were spent in Clontarf, in north Dublin. Both of his parents were, and still are, GPs. His mother, Geraldine, keeps the whole family in order, and is very much the boss of the house. Brian was the youngest of three children, with two sisters – Jules, a nurse, and Sue, who is two years younger, and works in event management along with doing a bit of radio work.

The family are close-knit and to this day they spend Sundays together whenever possible. At the meal table nobody gets more than anybody else. The girls aren't slow to tell Brian if the dishwasher needs filling, and the closeness and security of his family unit has undoubtedly helped to keep his feet on the ground and stop him becoming too big for his boots.

Even from a young age, Brian was showing signs of having a strong work ethic. As a child he hung a golf ball from a tree in the garden and would spend hours thwacking the ball with one of his dad's clubs. Frank said he didn't think his son was showing signs of madness, but was learning to develop his hand–eye co-ordination.

In those days, Frank kept a greenhouse of which he was very proud. If anyone broke a window with a stone they would be in big trouble. Do it with a ball, though, and it was in a good cause!

The garden was full of balls in those days. Golf balls, tennis balls, Gaelic footballs, soccer balls. Brian's first hero was footballer Mark Hughes, who he admired for his attitude as much as his ability. Tap-ins were never his style. Brian was a big Manchester United fan from a young age, but he was never much of a one for posters. As a child, he was always someone who kept his feelings very close to his chest. He was never an exhibitionist, and everything was always under control, with all things in sensible proportions. So far as the nature of his personality went, little changed as he grew into an adult.

Yet there was another side to him, a side that was fiercely competitive even as a young child. At the age of around 13 or 14, he was playing a round of golf with his father at Royal Dublin. They were playing the 10th, a par four, where you have to hit the ball across a mound, but there's a hollow to the left, and if you get it in there you seldom make par. Brian hit his tee shot straight into the mound. His father told him that he would give him 20 pounds if he made a par from there. So Brian responded by hitting a three-iron, followed by a chip to 10 feet before sinking the put. It was clear that Brian had a massive in-built determination.

As he grew up, he had his share of difficulties. A severe astigmatism – when the shape of the eyeball is not truly spherical – meant he could not keep contact lenses in, and he was chronically short-sighted, meaning he has always needed glasses for reading.

He was painfully shy throughout his childhood, and his parents found it a real struggle to get him to come out of his shell. That was the main reason he was sent to Blackrock College in Dublin, a fee-paying Catholic secondary school, which provided an education to several rugby stars including Alain Rolland, as well as other famous people such as the comedian and actor Ardal O'Hanlon. There was something about that school that appealed to Brian's parents. Children walked out of there with their shoulders pinned back and their heads held high. This was exactly what their son needed.

It didn't take long for the school to make an impact on Brian. In his second year he was elected as a class rep, a first taste of leadership for a future Ireland captain. His passion for sport continued to grow during his time here. Someone had seen him playing football (soccer) in the Community Games and encouraged him to join Trinity Boys, but at Blackrock he found rugby.

The summer before he started at Blackrock, he watched the 1991 Rugby World Cup on television. When he saw Michael Jones, the All Black flanker, Mark Hughes was relegated from top spot in his list of heroes. Brian watched with awe at what Jones could do. He was a back and a forward rolled into one combining great skill and superb running skills. He could tackle and mix it when it came to the rough stuff as well. Brian had found his role model.

However, when it came to his own development, things were a bit slow to begin with. Alan MacGinty, his school principal, left him off the Junior Cup team, on the grounds that he was tiny. That decision has haunted Alan ever since.

The only rugby Brian played in 1994 was with the under-16s at Clontarf. They won their league and that summer came the trip to Wales. Hugh Fanning, the coach, made some throwaway remark to Brian along the lines of: 'Don't forget to send me a postcard when you play for the Lions'. Seven years later, the card was in the post.

From then on, his talent began to shine through and, in 1996, while still at Blackrock, he was capped by Ireland Schools three times.

Legend surrounds his performance against Clongowes, in what was his last schools match. The Blackrock senior team were trailing as the clock ran down. Four times in the last five minutes, Brian tried to rescue the match with drop-goal attempts. One soared right over the top of the posts. Another hit the woodwork and bounced back into play, and Blackrock lost the game. This was a bitter pill to swallow, but learning to accept defeat with dignity was, unfortunately, something he would have to get used to as a sportsman.

Even at this stage, people were describing Brian as the new Brendan Mullin, who was considered by many to be the greatest Irish centre of recent times. After being something of a slow developer, or, perhaps more specifically, a slow grower, his skilful hands and ability to change gear quickly made him a real one to watch for the future.

At under-19 level, Brian was selected for the Ireland squad to play in the 1998 IRB under-19s World Championship in France, under the stewardship of respected coach Mike Ruddock. This tournament would have a profound effect on his career. By Brian's own admission, there is no comparing the standard of the under-19s with senior rugby, which he says is 100 times better, but the opportunity to play in this tournament provided an important stepping stone and a chance for him to impress in front of some important people. And he was involved in some memorable matches in that tournament.

There was the quarter-final against South Africa, when Ireland were 17–0 down and battled back to make it 17–17. It eventually went to penalty kicks before Ireland won those on a technicality because South Africa had used a player that hadn't finished the game as one of their five kickers. Ireland had lost the shoot-out 4–3, and Brian had taken one of the penalties and missed. Brian initially thought he had cost his side dear; until the technicality with the South African kicker was noticed, Brian was experiencing his first major low as a rugby player.

In the final, Ireland beat France 18–0 in Toulouse. Certainly, it was a team effort and everyone deserved credit for their remarkable achievement that day, but little did Brian know that he had caught the eye of some highly influential people and he was just a year away from playing for the Ireland senior team. Other notable names playing that day included Donncha O'Callaghan and Paddy Wallace.

Despite making remarkably rapid progress as a rugby player, Brian's parents were keen for him to gain qualifications as a back-up should something go wrong. His father knew only too well that his gifted son was only one nasty injury or one piece of bad luck away from being unable to play rugby again, and he was keen for him to have something for him to fall back on should this happen.

For this reason, Brian attended University College, Dublin on a scholarship. While at the college, he gained a diploma in sports management, but it was for his progress as a rugby player that his time there will be best remembered. Under Director of Rugby John McLean, he first made the under-20 side, before being promoted to the senior squad at the end of his first year.

Meanwhile, the Ireland squad were undergoing something of a revolution under Kiwi coach Warren Gatland, who was professionalising the entire setup to bring it into step with the modern era, while building a team that would, in time, compete with the world's very best. This meant breaking in players now who would form part of the Ireland side for the next decade, giving them a chance to know each other as players and as people early in the day.

Brian made his under-21 debut in February 1999, and went on to gain four caps. However, Warren clearly knew he had something very special when, incredibly, he called Brian into his senior squad for the Six Nations match against Italy. This was before he had even made his club debut for Leinster, which would not come until the August of that year. Brian's job that day was just to keep the bench warm, but he retained his place in the squad for the summer tour of Australia, and, on 12 June 1999, at the age of just 20, he made his senior debut for Ireland against the Wallabies in the first Test in Brisbane.

This match certainly wasn't Irish rugby's finest hour, as they crashed to a record 46–10 defeat, with Tiaan Strauss scoring a hat-trick of tries, but Brian certainly made his presence felt on the field that day and helped Ireland claim a fine consolation try when he, along with Connor O'Shea, dragged deep into Australian territory before Kevin Maggs finished off an impressive move.

He was far from the finished article, and still had a lot of growing up to do both in terms of his physique and in the development of his rugby skills, but, by showing what he was made of that day, he sealed his place in the Ireland team for the foreseeable future at least.

On 7 August 1999, Brian finally made his debut for Leinster, playing in an Interprovincial game against arch rivals Munster. Once again, Brian was on the losing side as they fell to a 31–20 defeat at Temple Hill.

Brian's development as a player was rapid, and in the Six Nations Championship of 2000 he showed how good he was when he took to the field in what was to be a very special game of rugby in Paris. However, the game started disastrously for Ireland when David Bory scored France's first try in the left corner after just 47 seconds. Or so they thought. Touch judge Jim Fleming ruled the final pass to be forward, but the warning was clear. This was a French side that meant business and would be tough to break down. Gérald Merceron soon put France 6–0 ahead, after Ireland were caught offside twice in as many minutes.

The first quarter of the game was a disaster for Ireland, but the game was about to change dramatically thanks largely to Brian's breathtaking efforts. He firstly collected the ball well from a French drop-out and Peter Stringer and Peter Clohessy drove into the ensuing ruck. It sent the home side backwards and there was little to stop Brian when he appeared in the move for the second time to touch down underneath the posts.

The home side soon hit back when scrum-half Christophe Laussucq scored following a quick tap penalty. In a match of blistering pace, Kieron Dawson then came close to replying, but knocked on as he touched over for Ireland on the left.

Early in the second half, Merceron kicked over a long penalty which saw the beginning of a period of play dominated by the home side, and it wasn't long before Merceron kicked over another penalty from right in front of the posts to stretch the French lead to 12 points.

Warren decided to bring on Paddy Johns to give experience to the flagging Irish pack, and his presence soon rubbed off on Brian. Some quality interplay between him and Rob Henderson saw him score his second of the game, silencing the French crowd. Ronan O'Gara converted to cut the lead to just six points. Although still relatively inexperienced at this level, Brian sensed this game was very winnable.

Disaster struck when Johns received a yellow card for blatantly lying on the ball. He left the field to French cheers as Merceron again increased the home lead. Warren then decided to replace Ronan with the experienced David Humphreys, who almost immediately scored a superb 40-metre penalty, but Ireland were caught offside far too often and Merceron soon put over another penalty of his own. The game looked to be heading firmly in the home side's direction, and it looked as though Ireland's appalling track record in France was going to remain. The last time they had won here was in 1972. Cue Brian O'Driscoll.

The French had been caught offside, after blatantly diving through a ruck. But an inspired piece of refereeing from Paul Honnis gave Stringer the opportunity to sidestep his way through a host of French tacklers, before offloading to Brian who went charging towards the try-line and secured his hat-trick. With just three minutes remaining, Humphreys converted to give Ireland a two-point lead. They managed to hang on, and won the game 27–25.

In the post-match interviews, Brian was typically shy and humble and heaped praise on David Humphreys's brave efforts. In Brian's eyes, David had been the hero of the day and he was keen to take the attention away from his own performance, which had just given Irish rugby one of the proudest days in its long history.

The Irish rugby fans had known that young Brian was good, but until that day they had not realised just how special he was. And they also had to remember that he was just 21 years of age, and there was plenty of room for improvement yet. Even people who didn't really follow rugby knew who Brian was after this. He was a true national hero and, even if he never played another game of rugby in his life, his would be a name they would never forget.

For Brian, life would never be the same again. From now on, media interest in every aspect of his life would be something he was just going to have to get used to. He was still very much a shy young man, and this was something he didn't always appreciate. But there would be an upside to it. All this attention would inevitably mean that there would be sponsorship opportunities and chances to make a great deal of money by having his name associated with big brands.

While Brian's progress remained rapid over the next few years, the same could not be said of the Ireland team. Warren was playing the long game, and his focus was more on the future than the present. The actions he was taking to professionalise Irish rugby would not bear fruit for several more years, and, on the pitch, his priority was to get his crop of talented youngsters used to playing together now, as they would form the nucleus of the team for the next decade. The price they would inevitably have to pay for this was that success would not be instant; on paper, the scorelines in big matches over the next few years were not pleasant reading and the prospect of picking up major trophies seemed a long way off.

Brian consolidated his excellent performance against France by playing consistently well for club and country over the next 12 months, and this led to him receiving a call-up to the Lions squad to tour Australia in the summer of 2001. Brian knew that there was still massive room for improvement in his game and there was still plenty of work to be done, but he knew this was an opportunity to impress on the world stage that he could not afford to miss.

The Lions were coached by Kiwi Graham Henry, who had experienced mixed fortunes as Wales coach over the previous few years. Brian and Graham did not enjoy an especially warm relationship during the tour; the main bone of contention being the importance of the preparation of the players for the midweek sides compared to those playing in the tests. The full extent of the disagreement that existed between Brian and Graham would not fully come to light for another four years.

However, Brian possessed undoubted talent and he was selected to play in all three Tests. It was in the first Test that he really made his presence felt, where he helped the Lions to a memorable win against the Wallabies.

The Lions looked firmly in control from the third minute when Jason Robinson scored in the corner. Brian's first major act as a Lions player came on 11 minutes, and it wasn't to be one of his finer moments. Rob Henderson tried passing to Brian, but it was intercepted by Joe Roff who almost broke free for the Wallabies.

He more than made up for any blame that could have

been attributed to him in that move in the 32nd minute when he ripped the Australian defence to shreds in spectacular fashion before off-loading to Jason Robinson who drew Andrew Walker, waited, and sent Dafydd James in at the corner for a wonderful score.

However, it was in the second half when the Lions really turned on the class. With a slender 12–3 lead, the Lions could have been forgiven for going on the defensive. Instead, they ripped into the Wallaby rearguard like men possessed.

The forwards maintained a rock-solid base 30 yards out. Jonny Wilkinson fed the ball to Brian and he smashed through the Aussie back-line like a supercharged tank and crashed over the line to send the 12,000 Lions fans in the Gabba crowd into raptures. Brian had shown his class on the world stage with a memorable try.

From then on, the game looked in the bag in a display of free-flowing, open rugby at its best and a further try from Scott Quinnell helped seal a 29–13 win for the Lions. Brian was pivotal in this victory and was playing like a man with far more experience than his 22 years would suggest. Captain Martin Johnson was full of praise for Brian's efforts, and described the game as one of the best he had ever been involved with or seen.

However, this was to be his best rugby of the tour. In the remaining two Tests, the Lions lost momentum and some of Graham Henry's preparation methods came into question as the unhappy atmosphere in the camp spilled over into the media, particularly from the newspaper columns of Matt Dawson and Austin Healey. It was even suggested by the media that a number of players were preparing to leave the tour early. In the months that followed, it became clear that the tour was not a happy one, with Henry saying in his own tour diary that he felt 'betrayed' by several players, namely those who gave accounts of the inner workings of the camp in their lucrative newspaper columns.

In the second Test at the Telstra Dome, Brian managed to break through the Australian line on a number of occasions but didn't receive the backup needed to capitalise upon his efforts, and the Lions suffered a humiliating 29–14 defeat.

In the final Test, Brian's only major contribution to the game was when he was on the receiving end of a high tackle from Herbert, which sent him crashing to the ground. The game was competitive and there was rarely more than a score in it, but ultimately the Lions were the poorer side and fell to a 29–23 defeat, handing Australia the series in the process.

The series was among the most competitive in history, and Brian had been one of the shining lights of the Lions team. He was only 22 years old and there was still a lot of room for improvement, but already he had established himself as one of the best centres in the world and had shown he was unfazed by the big occasion.

Yet in the months that followed the tour, his career saw something of a blip and he was far from at his best for the remainder of the year. Maybe something had to give. His life had changed beyond all recognition in a relatively short space of time. He had gone from being a shy, unassuming schoolboy to rugby superstar and national hero. All of this was going on while he was still in the process of becoming an adult, and it's arguable that people were expecting too much of him and the pressure was beginning to tell.

When the Six Nations came around the following spring, Brian returned to form in spectacular fashion, with Ireland's third match against Scotland proving to be one of the highlights of his career. The Ireland team took to the field at Lansdowne Road, eager to make amends for the catastrophic defeat to England they had suffered in the last round of matches.

Ireland kept Scotland pinned in their own half for the first 10 minutes, but their only reward came in the first minute through a Humphreys penalty. Gregor Townsend eventually relieved the pressure with a bombshell clearance and, when Mick Galwey fell over at a ruck, Brendan Laney levelled from 35 metres out. Laney kicked another one over just four minutes later to put Scotland in front.

Scotland, playing with the strong breeze, were putting

together some excellent passages of keep-ball which had the Irish defence scrambling. The pressure paid off for the visitors when Laney put his third penalty over in the 22nd minute. Ireland were looking down-and-out, but Brian was about to return to form in spectacular fashion and turn the game in his country's favour.

Just three minutes after Laney's penalty, Stringer whipped the ball away left to Humphreys who put Brian through a yawning gap as the Scottish defence was caught by the decoy run of Kevin Maggs. At last, Brian's poor run of form seemed to be over, and this special try seemed to help him put the demons that had haunted him since the previous summer to bed.

Brian seemed psyched up and ready to take on the world, back to his most bold, confident and deadly, and just seven minutes later he was at the centre of the action once more. He started the move with a powerful kick upfield, and then helped finish things off when his long pass drifted wide to left-wing Shane Horgan, who ran in unaccompanied.

More was to follow before half-time when the Scotland midfield dropped the ball in the home 22. Up stepped Brian who moved in swiftly to scoop it up and sprint all the way in. Humphreys added the conversion. Suddenly, all Brian's problems with confidence seemed like ancient history. This was more like the Drico who scored a hat-trick against France.

Laney reduced the Scots' deficit with a penalty either side of half-time, before Humphreys relieved some of the pressure now being put on Ireland with two rifled penalties, passing Michael Kiernan's record of 308 points for his country in the process.

With 15 minutes remaining, Ireland added another try when the Scottish midfield clumsily dropped the ball for the umpteenth time in the match, allowing Horgan to feed Humphreys who in turn switched direction for Simon Easterby to glide in.

Scotland scored a consolation try but it was Brian who was to have the final word on the game, when a quick ball from an Irish scrum allowed him to dart between Andrew Henderson and James McLaren, to score his second Six Nations hat-trick and seal Ireland's only second victory over Scotland in 15 matches, by a comfortable 43–22 margin. Brian O'Driscoll was back in business.

As for the Ireland team itself, it soon became clear that this was still very much a side in transition. Frustration at the lack of consistency had seen Warren sacked as coach and he had been replaced by his assistant, Eddie O'Sullivan. Consistency was still very much a problem. On the one hand, they had beaten Wales and Scotland, yet on other days they had suffered humiliating defeats at the hands of England and France.

Longstanding Ireland captain Keith Wood announced

his retirement after the autumn internationals of 2002. In Eddie's mind, Brian was the natural and most obvious successor to Keith, and the announcement that Brian would be captaining Ireland in the 2003 Six Nations surprised few. It is true that, at just 24 years of age, he lacked the kind of experience most previous captains had seen, but there were clearly many good reasons why Brian was ready for the job.

Mainly, Eddie's eye was very much on the future. Yes, there was no reason why Ireland shouldn't be serious contenders for the upcoming Six Nations, but there were a crop of truly outstanding players on the horizon who would not reach their peak for another few years. Like his predecessor, Eddie believed in getting them used to playing together early on, so that, when they were all at the top of their games in a few years' time, they would know one another's games inside out.

Brian was still very much an improving player. Incredibly, he still had his critics. There were, for instance, still those who believed his kicking game was not up to scratch, yet this previous weakness had come on in leaps and bounds over the previous 12 months. In reality, Eddie knew that Brian had what it took to make an outstanding captain, despite his relatively young age. He had shown battling qualities in so many Ireland performances to date and, despite his reserved and humble personality, was proving to be a ruthless warrior on the pitch.

Every serious rugby fan in the world now acknowledged that he was one of the world's greatest players, and was still getting better all the time. The Ireland fans had taken him to their hearts, so much so that T-shirts bearing the slogans 'In B.OD We Trust' were soon printed following his appointment as captain and have remained popular at Ireland matches ever since.

In his first Six Nations as captain, Brian led Ireland to four wins out of the first four matches, which included an impressive try of his own against Italy. The scene was set for a Grand Slam decider at Lansdowne Road against a powerful England side. On the day, Ireland struggled to get going and were simply outclassed by the more mature England side, and, despite Brian and Geordan Murphy testing the resolve of the England defence early on, the result never looked in any doubt and England secured a walloping 42–6 victory. After the game, Brian told the press that slowly, but surely, they were getting there and it was only going to be a matter of time before Ireland ranked among the world's greatest sides. For him, it was disappointing to lose the game but he was still hugely optimistic for the future, as he knew the sheer quality of the young players coming through.

This defeat set alarm bells ringing in certain quarters and not everybody at the IRFU was willing to play the 'long game' that Eddie and Brian were committed to.

Keith Wood, who had barely even featured for his club Harlequins during the season, was coaxed out of international retirement. It was decided that he, rather than Brian, should lead Ireland in the upcoming World Cup, which was to be his third as a player.

Brian could easily have felt cheated of the opportunity to captain his country in the World Cup, but instead he stuck his head down and quietly got on with the job, knowing that, once the tournament was over, Keith would be off the scene for good and the role of captain would be his once more. This decision was certainly a controversial one, as it went against the youth-based ethos that Eddie had subscribed to throughout his tenure so far. Yet it was the long, patient game that had cost Warren his job and the powers that be weren't willing to wait much longer for Ireland to become serious contenders. This meant that it was Keith's job to add some much-needed experience to this very young squad.

The first three matches of the tournament saw Ireland notch up convincing victories against Romania and Namibia in the Pool stages, before defeating a resilient Argentina by a single point thanks to a try from Alan Quinlan. Brian made his presence felt in Ireland's final group game against Australia. In the second half, with his side 14–6 down, he scored one of the most memorable tries of his career to date. The video referee was brought in to judge whether the Irish ace had touched the ball down in the left corner before his feet went into touch, but the Irish faithful inside the stadium were never in any doubt.

Ronan added the conversion, to put Ireland within a point of the world champions. Elton Flatley kicked another penalty to make the gap four points, but a drop goal from Brian with 13 minutes to play kept Ireland in the hunt. Unfortunately, Australia were just that little bit too strong for them and the more experienced side managed to hang on for victory.

Despite the defeat, Ireland had done enough in their earlier matches and set up a mouth-watering quarter-final clash against France. Although Ireland were the underdogs, Brian had remembered how his side had beaten France 15–12 in a closely fought match in Dublin during the Six Nations and knew this game was very winnable.

However, come the day, the French stormed to a 27–0 lead at half-time and amassed four tries in the process. Even so, Brian was at the top of his game and things could have been so much worse for the Irish had he not been playing. Early on, he made a crucial last-gasp tackle on a flying Tony Marsh to deny him an almost certain try.

Crenca scored France's fourth try inside the first 10 minutes of the second period, effectively ending the game as a contest, but Ireland soon got on the scoreboard with a try from Kevin Maggs. This was now an exercise in damage limitation, and Brian was clearly keen to give the thousands of Irish fans at least some momentum they could be proud of from this game.

Sure enough, Brian delivered Ireland's second consolation try when he got a touch on Humphreys's grubber kick, and on the final whistle he added a second to bring respectability to the scoreline, which read France 43 Ireland 21. Things would have been a lot worse without Brian.

Ireland's World Cup had been typical of the sort of form they had been showing over the past year. On occasions, they looked like they could beat any team in the world yet they were a young squad and on the really big occasions their lack of experience and squad depth really did show, but at the same time it was clear that this side was going to be one to watch for the future.

As expected, Keith Wood announced his retirement from rugby immediately after Ireland's defeat to France, and Brian was immediately reinstated as captain for the Six Nations campaign in the spring.

Ironically, Ireland had to face France in Paris in the first round of fixtures, and unfortunately for Brian the game turned out to be a recurring nightmare of the World Cup quarter-final as Ireland crashed to a 35–17 defeat in similar style to their World Cup exit. The Grand Slam chance may have been lost, but this was an

Ireland side that needed to show the world that they were maturing fast and that the day when they would be winning major trophies was near.

At home to a lacklustre Wales side, Brian turned on the class, scoring two of Ireland's six tries as they stormed to a commanding 36–15 victory. Next up came an away match against the newly crowned world champions, England, who had crushed Italy and Scotland in their opening two fixtures, despite having to do without an injured Jonny Wilkinson and a number of retirements following the World Cup triumph.

England scored the only try of the first half through Matt Dawson but some superb kicking from Ronan saw the visitors take a 12–10 lead at the break. However, England came out firing in the second half and Ben Cohen went over only for the video referee to rule out the try for a double movement. This seemed to inspire Brian and within minutes he made a superb break, the ball was spread wide and Leinster full-back Girvan Dempsey crossed over in the corner. Ronan converted, and England could only offer a Paul Grayson penalty in response, giving Ireland an incredible 19–12 victory against the world champions, thanks largely to some stubborn and determined defending.

After the game, Brian could not hide his delight and the normally reserved and quiet Ireland captain could not wait to tell the world that this side had arrived on the world rugby scene and meant business. At long last, the young team that had shown so much promise had finally delivered the goods.

A fortnight later, Ireland consolidated their excellent performance against England when Brian guided his side to a 19–3 home win against Italy, which included a try of his own. Going into the final round of fixtures, the Triple Crown was still on, but, realistically, the Championship was out of the question unless England managed to thrash France by an enormous margin. Instead, Brian had to focus all his attentions on beating Scotland at Lansdowne Road. The game also saw Brian notch up his 50th cap for Ireland at the age of just 25. He was keen to make this a day for all Irish rugby fans to remember, a day when they finally had a trophy to parade around their historic home ground, which was the oldest in the world.

The home side had a nervy first period against a fired-up Scotland team but Geordan Murphy's try just before the break gave Ireland a 16–9 lead; however, the visitors did level the scores with an Ali Hogg try on 48 minutes. This Scotland side was clearly keen on causing an upset after a dreadful tournament to date. However, three tries in the final 24 minutes, including a second for Gordon D'Arcy, sealed the win for Ireland. The final quarter of the game was hardly vintage rugby from either side, but Ireland had done enough.

Finally, Ireland had something to show for their efforts: the Triple Crown. After years of showing promise but failing on the big occasion, this was a massive sign that things were finally starting to come together for this promising young squad. The final game was a quiet one by Brian's standards, but his impact in earlier matches had been enormous and his efforts as both player and captain had been pivotal in contributing to Ireland's historic achievement.

Brian celebrated with a night at Kehoe's Bar in Dublin. This was a day to remember. But Brian was also aware that, from now on, this was the minimum requirement, and that next year, and thereafter, the fans expected even better from the team.

That autumn, Brian led his team out at Lansdowne Road to face a South Africa side that had been rejuvenated under the stewardship of coach Jake White. Ronan scored all Ireland's points as they beat the Southern Hemisphere giants 17–12, but the win was in no small part down to Brian's no-nonsense approach from start to finish. Ireland had defended and tackled superbly and richly deserved this victory. They consolidated this with an expected thrashing of the USA, before ending the autumn series by beating a rapidly improving Argentina side 21–19, with Ronan providing all the points once again.

Brian might not have managed to get his name on the

scoresheet against South Africa and Argentina, but he had steered Ireland to two memorable victories, and had led by example by giving his best from start to finish. After a shaky start, 2004 had ended on a high, and it seemed that, after over five years of preparation, this Ireland side had finally come of age. Things were not perfect, and a number of players were far from the finished article, but it was clear that Ireland were to be a major force in world rugby in the years ahead. The years of patient preparation had finally paid off, and the reality was that Brian was now the captain of one of the world's best rugby teams.

Brian's status as one of the world's greatest centres was secure, but he was quickly developing a reputation as a strong leader and great motivator of those around him. With such status comes increased responsibility and raised expectations, and Brian knew that the year ahead would be one of the most important of his life.

# CHAPTER 2

# COMING OF AGE

The following year, 2005, was always going to be pivotal in Brian's career. He was now 25 years old, and the previous few years had seen him mature rapidly as a person; the stature and esteem in which he was held by both his team-mates and rugby fans in Ireland and beyond had risen sharply.

On paper, it looked like being a gruelling 12 months, and expectations were high. Leinster were in with a very real chance of winning the Heineken Cup. The Ireland team looked stronger than ever, and fans were expecting nothing less than their country capturing their first Grand Slam in 57 years.

There was to be no summer break. Brian would

undoubtedly be selected for the Lions tour to New Zealand, where they would be looking to win a Test Series against the All Blacks for only the second time.

The year got off to a bad start, when on the evening of New Year's Day Brian lined up for Leinster to take on old rivals Munster at Musgrave Park. Brian had never found it difficult to psych himself up for matches against Munster, and was fully prepared for the challenging 80 minutes that lay ahead. This was his chance to get an important year off to the best possible start, and he didn't want to let the opportunity slip through his hands without a fight.

With both sides at full strength and Munster in superb form, it proved to be a typically physical encounter between the traditional rivals, which saw Irish fly-half Ronan O'Gara breaking a bone in his right hand, leaving a serious question mark over whether he would be available for the early Six Nations fixtures which were now only a month away.

Leinster lost the game 19–13, and Brian's year had got off to the worst possible start as far as he was concerned. Losing is never pleasant, but, with rivalry between the two provinces so intense, the defeat was especially painful to take.

However, Brian had no time to dwell on this defeat as the following week he had to travel to Bath as Leinster's quest for Heineken Cup glory continued. Things didn't look good and with four minutes to go Leinster were trailing 23–13. But there was still time to turn it around, and a late surge saw tries from David Holwell and Malcolm O'Kelly to make it 27–23 at the end.

Bath coach John Connolly knew his team had thrown the game away, and was quick to praise Brian's contribution. In a post-match interview with the BBC, he said, 'The guys were focused, the effort was phenomenal but the odd mistake cost us the game and the players are incredibly disappointed. Any team that has Brian O'Driscoll and up to six potential Lions in their line-up always has a chance.'

But Brian was far from happy with his performance in the game, and cursed himself for a sloppy pass he made to Girvan Dempsey early on that probably cost his team a try. That said, a win is a win and Brian's efforts that day played no small part in Leinster's stunning turnaround in the final few minutes.

In the professional era, matches come thick and fast and there is little time to dwell on defeats or revel in victories. Within a week, Brian would be meeting up with the Ireland squad as they prepared for their Six Nations campaign. On 21 January, just two days before the squad was due to meet, Brian should have been celebrating his 26th birthday. Instead, he opted for a quiet day, knowing that this really wasn't the time for a night's boozing with mates. If he and Ireland were serious about completing the Grand Slam, they had to be in the peak of physical fitness, and this meant making sacrifices early on.

Brian enjoyed playing with an iPod given to him by O2, one of Ireland's sponsors, before heading to the barber's to cut off the blond locks he had been sporting in favour of a short-back-and-sides look. A serious haircut for a serious man. There was no clowning around now, and Brian used this small gesture as a statement of intent for the challenges that lay ahead.

Two days later, and Brian joined the Ireland squad at the City West hotel in Dublin. This would be his base until the end of the Six Nations.

From now on, each day's activities would run to a strict schedule. Essentially this meant a daily ritual of eating, training and sleeping. As usual, Brian did not enjoy the prospect of having to be away from home for such a long period of time. The novelty of having everything laid on for him never took long to wear off. He felt the daily training ritual was not especially different to that he underwent at home and he much preferred to be around those closest to him, especially with such a long build-up to the first game of the Six Nations.

Brian has gone on record as saying that he doesn't necessarily believe that spending long periods together as a squad is the best way to prepare for a game. He points out that in the 1970s international sides put together breathtaking performances on the back of a maximum of just two days together.

It's easy to see where he's coming from, but in the professional era few would argue that the highest levels of fitness and the correct diet are essential in preparing for big games and that joining together as a squad early on plays an important part in getting this right. They might not enjoy being away from those closest to them for so long, but it is a fact of life for the modern international rugby player.

Brian's left-shoulder injury, sustained early in his career, soon came back to haunt him in the days that followed and he wasn't able to train as rigorously as he would have liked. After each training session, he would apply an electro-magnetic TENS pain-relief gadget to his shoulder to alleviate the persistent problem. This was far from ideal preparation for the tournament.

Brian was the first to put his problems into perspective. Irritating though this was, it was nothing compared to those suffering the effects of the Tsunami disaster just a few weeks earlier, and watching the terrible pictures of the aftermath from his hotel room helped him realise this.

Being captain, and being the biggest 'celebrity' in the squad, meant Brian had to do more than his fair share of media work in the lead-up to the tournament. He has never been a natural extrovert and shyness was a problem early on in his career, with his personality never coming across on television. Things had improved as he grew into the captaincy, and by now Brian's approach to interviews was every bit as professional as his approach to other aspects of being a rugby player.

On the day of the Six Nations press launch, Brian had to make himself available for a number of interviews with journalists from various organisations from around the world. This in itself proved something of a challenge. He was expected to treat each interview with the seriousness of the last one. In all likelihood, this meant being asked exactly the same questions as before, which meant having to give exactly the same answers.

Brian always stuck to the official party line, never speaking out of turn. He knew full well that making one light-hearted comment or poking a bit of fun at the opposition could easily be taken out of context and backfire on him spectacularly, which was exactly what had happened to him the previous year.

In an interview before the Ireland–England game, Brian had made a comment along the lines that an Ireland win would give the prawn-sandwich brigade at Twickenham something to choke on.

Of course, the Celtic nations love nothing more than winding up the 'posh boys' of England and his remarks went down well back home. Brian was simply parodying comments made by Roy Keane about Manchester

United's corporate 'supporters' some years previously. But his rather lame attempt at humour certainly seemed to psych up his opponents. Lawrence Dallaglio seemed to take it very personally and appeared more angry than usual as he took to the field that day. The remark was blown out of all proportion but it certainly seemed to stick and speculation was rife that it had done serious damage to Brian's relationship with Sir Clive Woodward.

In the context of those remarks, it came as a huge surprise to Brian when, in the middle of his preparations for the Six Nations, he received a phone call from Clive inviting him to his home in Henley for a chat about the upcoming Lions tour. Brian had no idea what this could mean. Yes, the press had grossly exaggerated the extent of his rift with Clive but he could hardly be described as one of his closest confidants.

Not knowing what to expect, Brian took a flight to Heathrow where Clive picked him up at Arrivals and drove him to his sublime home. The whole evening turned out to be a very relaxed and friendly occasion. The two men just talked frankly about the upcoming Lions tour, with Clive appearing to take a keen interest in which players Brian rated. The alleged falling out of 12 months previously suddenly felt like a million years ago. Then the true purpose of the meeting was revealed.

Clive asked Brian how he felt about captaining the Lions. It was phrased as a hypothetical question rather than an offer, but Brian knew exactly what this meant. The hairs stood up on the back of his neck, and, as he put it, his whole rugby career flashed before him. To captain the Lions is almost certainly the greatest honour any rugby player from Britain or Ireland could ever receive, and now it was practically being offered on a plate to Brian. He answered the question with an enthusiastic 'Yes' before going on to say that he was a big believer in the Martin Johnson style of captaincy, but he wasn't looking to be a clone of him.

The rest of the evening was spent discussing a strategy for the tour. Both men agreed that the tour of New Zealand should be fun. They both knew full well that many players didn't enjoy the 2001 Lions tour of Australia. This was partly due to a large number of players being marginalised in the midweek side early on. Both men agreed that back then the Lions simply needed more back-room staff to do the job properly. Clive agreed to set up two different teams of coaches and medics. There was obviously no way every member of the squad could play in the Test team, but making every player feel valued and properly supported was vital in making for a happy, coherent squad.

With more emphasis on fun, Clive made sure the tour allowed time to absorb the country and the culture, as well as allowing for a few decent nights out. This didn't have to mean heavy drinking sessions, but it did mean avoiding a siege mentality within the camp. They were away from home for a long time, and making the tour an enjoyable experience was now considered an important aspect of making it a success on the field. After all, if they were playing a series of matches at home with that length of gap in between, there would certainly be space made for some 'down time'.

At the end of their meeting, Clive made it clear that he would not be making any final decision on the captaincy until after the Six Nations. But Brian was aware that it was now his to lose, and that, if he remained professional in his leadership of Ireland, the job would be his.

The following day saw the official media launch of the Six Nations in London. Brian was growing sick and tired of constant interviews, press gatherings and posing for pictures by now. The build-up seemed never ending but this was just something he had to learn to put up with. It came as part of the job and that was that.

Brian nevertheless coped well with the many interviews he had to do, until about halfway through the day when he got bored with repeating the same old lines to one journalist after another and decided to say something that would stir up a degree of controversy.

He commented that world champions England had lost their aura of invincibility. This was by no means an outrageous remark, since several former England captains had publicly said exactly the same thing in recent weeks. After all, the England team that would be taking to the field in the Six Nations was missing the likes of Martin Johnson, Jonny Wilkinson and Richard Hill, to name just three of the stars of their World Cup campaign.

Inevitably, the English press spun his words into a severe dig at the current England squad. The reality was that the squad were rebuilding in between World Cups and few could seriously deny that this was an England team in transition, but these remarks were pinned very firmly on Brian and he had to live with the fall-out that followed.

He knew that this would wind up several members of the England squad and that the best way to cope with this would be to fight fire with fire. Ireland had been made pre-tournament favourites and Brian employed the mentality of the All Blacks, who are favourites before just about every match they play. They then embrace this thought and build it into their preparation.

Ireland were pre-tournament favourites and had an experienced, yet developing squad, and, as captain, Brian saw no reason why they couldn't go on and take the Six Nations by storm.

The campaign was due to start with a trip to Italy. Brian decided to sit out Leinster's game against Gwent the week before so as not to aggravate his shoulder. This meant he hadn't had much match practice in the run-up to the Italy game, but he went for the lower-risk strategy of doing a full week's training instead.

The away trip to Italy was never going to be a walkover. They had come on in leaps and bounds since John Kirwan took over as coach and their days of being the whipping boys of the Six Nations were well and truly over. Worryingly for Brian, they tended to put in their best performance of the Championship in their first match. Italy were fresh, had prepared well and, as it was the first game, were generally free from any significant injury worries within the camp.

This was always likely to be a baptism of fire for Brian. A week before the match, a journalist who had known Brian for many years put it to him that he had matured as a person and would now handle comfortably the sort of situations that would have fazed the Brian O'Driscoll of five years previously. It was more a statement than a question. Brian had been captain for two years by now, but never before had he captained a team as well prepared and well balanced as this. It was up to him to lead by example. The time had come to deliver.

As expected, Italy didn't roll over easily on home soil. They took an early lead through a Luciano Orquera penalty after seven minutes. Italy had the better of the first quarter before a Ronan O'Gara penalty drew the scores level. With Ireland struggling to maintain possession, it looked like being a long, hard slog to get anything out of the game. Cue Brian O'Driscoll.

Just before the half-hour mark, he ran a dummy scissors and made a breathtaking outside break before passing to Geordan Murphy who scored in the corner. However, an Italian penalty followed, leaving Ireland trailing 9–8 at half-time.

In the second half, Brian really turned up the heat and led by example, and it was his break that set up Peter Stringer's try. For most of the second half, though, it looked as though Italy could quite easily have snatched the game as they tested the Irish defence time and time again. A Denis Hickie try made sure Ireland didn't lose the game, but it could hardly be described as a convincing victory. It was a sluggish performance by Ireland and the 28–17 scoreline was flattering to say the least.

Brian's predecessor as Ireland captain, Keith Wood, was working as a pundit for the BBC and said that if Brian hadn't been playing it could easily have been a different result. Worryingly, Brian picked up a hamstring injury in the last minute. There was no way Ireland could have lost the match that late on, but Brian took his dedication a tad too far by getting involved scrambling around with the pack in the final seconds. Judging by his team's performance on the day, he should have thought of the greater good and not taken any unnecessary risks.

## Coming of Age

Yet this was typical of Brian's character. He only knows how to play rugby one way, to get stuck in and stay involved for the whole 80 minutes. That night, and during the following morning, he nursed his injury with ice back at the hotel. All he could do was be as still as possible and get bored out of his mind sipping tea.

The flight home was delayed so Brian was left sitting around for even longer than he would have liked. Clive Woodward put in a call asking how bad the injury was. By now it seemed Brian would be laid off for weeks rather than months, and fingers crossed he would be ready to captain the Lions. But for now, there was no hiding the disappointment that he was unlikely to feature much more in Ireland's Six Nations campaign.

With the rest of the Ireland squad preparing for the next game against Scotland, Brian would spend the week working around the clock with the medics on his hamstring. It soon became clear to all in the Ireland camp that neither Brian nor Gordon D'Arcy was going to feature in the Scotland game, but this was to remain a closely guarded secret all week. After all, why put the Scotland squad at ease by giving them this crucial information sooner than they had to? It seemed far better to let them sweat a little. It was only when the Ireland squad left for Edinburgh on the Thursday that their secret was out.

Instead, Brian and Gordon were off on a little trip of

their own, to somewhere very different. On the Sunday, they were to fly out to the Cryotherapy Chambers in Spala, Poland, for five days' intensive treatment to try to get them fit for the England game.

During Warren Gatland's reign as Ireland coach, the whole squad had been to the complex for intensive training sessions. It is a gruelling, unforgiving place but the facilities there are state-of-the-art and leave nothing to chance.

It has a well-equipped fitness centre with some added bonuses, such as the ice chambers for cryotherapy, where they can set the temperature to minus 120 degrees, enabling you to triple your workload on any given day. The theory is that the extreme cold boosts your circulation and thereby flushes out the toxins that release chemicals into the system, such as lactic acid. Brian and Gordon hoped the experience would speed up their recovery by up to two weeks, allowing them both to take to the field against England.

Brian checked out of the City West hotel just as the rest of the of the squad headed for Edinburgh, and decided to spend a few days at home before flying off to Poland. He watched the Scotland game there with his sister Jules. Brian has never enjoyed watching matches he should be involved in and this was no exception.

As had been the case all too often in the recent past, Ireland got off to a sloppy start and Scotland took the lead through a Hugo Southwell try. However, the Ireland team recovered as the boys led by stand-in captain Paul O'Connell turned on the style. Ronan O'Gara was back on superb kicking form, and five superb tries saw Ireland come out 40–13 winners. In truth, the scoreline flattered the Scotland performance as Shane Horgan spilled the ball over the line in what was otherwise a great effort by him, and the Irish defence were superb throughout.

Brian flew out to Warsaw early on the Sunday morning, but getting there proved to be an adventure in itself. The IRFU had booked Brian and Gordon under different names to avoid drawing unwanted attention to their trip. Brian became Brendan O'Donovan and Gordon was Graham Delaney.

When Brian went to check in, he didn't know whether he should keep up the pretence or whether the ground crew were in on the scheme. When asked his name, Brian froze, as though it was a tricky question or he had something dodgy to hide, so he just gave a daft grin.

It didn't get any easier in the departure lounge. A middle-aged lady came up to him and asked him if he was the young actor in the O2 advert on television. Brian couldn't wait to get on board, put his earphones in and get back to sleep.

Upon landing in Warsaw, Brian and Gordon faced a two-hour drive to the complex. The journey wasn't particularly welcoming. The temperature was well below freezing and dirty snow was piled high on the sides of the road amid grim, barren scenery.

For the next four days, the two would undertake a punishing daily routine that usually included no fewer than three cryotherapy sessions per day, combined with fitness work and sessions in the pool, complete with bungee straps and cords. The cryotherapy sessions weren't a miracle cure by any means, but they did do a great deal to speed up the recovery process.

The challenge was to stay in the chamber for as long as you were able to. Medics were on hand to ensure the players did not stay in for longer than was safe, monitoring their blood pressure closely. At a stretch, Brian could manage eight minutes in the chamber.

At the end of each session, Brian would feel freezing cold and would hop straight on the exercise bike, working frantically to warm himself up. In the evenings, the two would go to a nearby restaurant with their translator. On the way back, it would be pitch black and there was sheet ice everywhere. Brian became very aware of the strange noises coming from the woodlands and felt that slipping on the ice and breaking a leg or being savaged by a pack of Polish wolves would be a strange way to bow out of the Six Nations. Brian hated being in Spala and found it a grim, miserable place, and wasn't sorry when his four-day stay was over. That said, the trip could be deemed successful. Brian was now well on the road to recovery and had lost half a stone in weight during the week.

The journey back to Warsaw airport proved even more miserable than the journey to Spala. A twin-carriaged bus slid out of control on a roundabout and Brian's taxi driver slammed into the side of the bus with an almighty thud. Luckily, nobody was seriously hurt but it was a frightening experience for Brian and Gordon to endure.

When he got back to Dublin, Brian received a number of text messages from his team-mates asking him how the trip had gone. He sent them sarcastic replies telling them Spala was gorgeous and that he was planning a holiday there in August. Most of the squad should probably have known better since so many of them had been there at some point over the previous few years.

A few days later, *The Times* reported that Paul O'Connell was about to be named as captain for the summer's Lions tour. Of course, those close to Brian knew different but it was still a closely guarded secret. Paul's captaincy of Ireland in Brian's absence had been well received and comparisons were regularly being made between him and Martin Johnson, as both players and personalities. Over breakfast that morning, the rest of the squad wound Paul up about the rumours, and told him to put in a good word to Sir Clive. Brian didn't take the reports too seriously, and knew he was still on course to captain the Lions.

That same day, Brian was declared fit to start against England the following weekend, but Gordon wasn't quite ready.

Brian didn't take any unnecessary risks in the days leading up to the game. Come the day, he remained cautious and was still quite worried that his hamstring could give at any time. Lansdowne Road is a notoriously cold place, and Brian knew that standing around for such a long time before the whistle blew was not going to be good for him.

Preliminaries there tended to take longer than at other grounds. The players were first presented to Ireland's President, Mary MacAleese, after which came the away team's anthem, followed by Ireland's two anthems. On a cold February day, this allowed more than enough time for Brian's hamstring to play up.

The game that followed will be talked about for decades. England had lost their two previous games and Ireland were on a high. The whole squad, Brian more than most, really believed they had what it took to crush England.

An early drop goal from Ronan gave Ireland a slender advantage but England took the lead with a try by Martin Corry. This only stirred Brian up even more. He was now more determined than ever to break England down and Ireland were on the charge for much of the rest of the first half, with Brian leading by example by trying to break through the English back row time and again.

However, it was referee Jonathan Kaplan who became the centre of attention as half-time approached. Mark Cueto thought he had scored after a Charlie Hodgson cross-field kick but Kaplan ruled that he had started in front of the kicker.

England were the stronger team at the start of the second half, and a rare Irish break-out gave Ronan a chance to kick at goal, which he missed. A Charlie Hodgson drop goal extended England's lead still further, but the tide of the game was about to change dramatically.

Ireland took control of possession and passed the ball around well. Geordan Murphy played a clever dummy on Hodgson, before passing over to Brian who touched down between the posts. Brian's hard work had paid off and his try was well deserved.

From then on, it was Ireland all the way. Some clumsy kicking from Ronan wasn't enough to dampen the spirits. Ireland had beaten England and had deserved to win. Several members of the English squad were less than gracious in defeat, and did their best to deflect attention away from their own shortcomings by blaming the referee for the result. Kaplan had disallowed 'tries' from Cueto and Josh Lewsey during the game, which, upon closer inspection, pretty much showed he had got the decision correct. If anything, Ireland were hard done by when Kaplan missed Danny Grewcock blocking Ronan on the edge of a ruck.

England coach Andy Robinson led the complaining in the post-match press conference. His team had now lost nine of their last fourteen matches under him and he knew he was under a lot of pressure.

It took several days before any member of the England squad owned up to the painful truth. Martin Corry admitted in an interview that England had 'stuffed up' and that the team, not the referee, were responsible for the defeat.

Brian's heavy involvement in this physical encounter left him feeling very sore the following day, but his hamstring had survived the ordeal and after a session in the pool that afternoon he realised he was in one piece and ready to prepare for the next challenge.

Next up were France at Lansdowne Road, who had just suffered a narrow defeat to Wales, despite playing some of the most exciting attacking rugby the Championship had seen in years.

Brian managed to squeeze in a trip to Twickenham for a North v South Tsunami benefit game. Although he was nominated captain, it would have been foolish to play in the game but his presence there certainly gave the event some welcome publicity. Clive Woodward was coaching the North side and had organised a team dinner, which gave Brian a chance to get to know some of his future

Lions team-mates in relaxed circumstances. Brian also had to shoot an advert for Adidas for the Lions tour. He had his reservations about doing the advert when the make-up of the final squad was far from certain, but by now a large part of him was growing to enjoy all the posing and hype these shoots provided. It certainly came as a welcome break from the City West hotel.

In the week that followed, the Grand Slam hype in the media just grew and grew. The squad, and Brian in particular, knew all along it wasn't out of the question, but the wider public were only just starting to cotton on to how good this Ireland side really was. However, this French side were good, and Ireland were going to have to overcome them without the likes of Horgan, D'Arcy and Maggs. This was always going to be a tough game.

It wasn't long before Brian was called upon to make his presence felt when after just two minutes he made a try-saving interception after Julien Laharrague went on the charge. A penalty kick from Ronan saw Ireland take an early lead, but France equalised with a drop goal just three minutes later.

Brian was on the receiving end of a high tackle from Yann Delaigue that gave Ronan the opportunity to restore Ireland's lead after 18 minutes. Yet again, France levelled the scores almost immediately after Simon Easterby was caught offside. French indiscipline allowed

Ronan to put his country 9–6 up after 25 minutes, but things were to go rapidly downhill from then on.

Just three minutes later, France put together a brilliant move that ended with a Christophe Dominici try, which was followed by another French try just a few minutes later after some shambolic Irish defending allowed Benoit Baby through to score, putting France 18–9 up at half-time.

Ireland restored some form of respectability early in the second half, courtesy of Ronan's reliable kicking; however, this was cancelled out by a French penalty after 61 minutes. Ireland were down and out, but Brian wasn't going to quit until the final whistle had been blown. With just eight minutes to play, and his side out of the game, he broke through three French tackles to score under the posts. Ronan duly converted, putting just two points between the teams, providing a nail-biting final few minutes of the game. Once again, the Irish defence leaked, allowing Dominici to score for France, sealing a 26–19 victory.

The Grand Slam dream was in tatters, leaving Brian at the lowest ebb he had ever felt in his professional career. He had done well enough in the game, and he knew his team had what it took to defeat the French. He also knew that a chance like this only came once in a generation for sides like his. He also had to accept his share of responsibility for the second French try, which was partly due to a sloppy error on his part.

## Coming of Age

Despite his disappointment, Brian knew he had a professional duty to remain positive for the post-match interviews. The Irish public saw the upcoming game against Wales as a Championship decider and they wanted to hear from Brian that there was still all to play for.

Coach Eddie O'Sullivan was as disappointed as any of his players, but he knew that there simply wasn't time to dwell on this defeat. He decided that the whole squad needed a two-day mini-break to take things easy and lighten the mood in the camp.

They stayed in the grounds of the City West for the duration of the break. There was golf for those who wanted it, as well as time for massage and sauna sessions. Brian decided to take the opportunity to enjoy a few lie-ins and lounge around for a while.

On the Thursday, the squad flew to Cardiff for the crunch-match against Wales. The sheer number of cameras flashing when they arrived at the airport reminded Brian that this was no ordinary game, and fans from both nations expected big things from their players in two days' time.

Wales had been breathtaking in the Championship thus far. Brian knew Wales coach Mike Ruddock well from his days at Leinster. In fact, it was Mike who had offered Brian his first-ever professional contract. Mike had got Wales playing attacking, running rugby, making

Wales a team that could give every nation on the planet a run for their money for the first time in two decades. Brian knew his side would have their work cut out in this massive game.

The day before the match, the squad tested out the Millennium Stadium pitch. Brian was taken aback by his impressive surroundings, and he said at the time that it put the state of Lansdowne Road to shame. He liked the atmosphere the ground could generate, but this was the professional era and Ireland was now a prosperous country that deserved a national rugby stadium far better than this.

Redevelopment was on the cards within the next few years, but there was talk that Ireland would have to play their games at Twickenham or Cardiff while the work was being carried out. This frustrated Brian, who thought the matches could be played at Croke Park, the home of Gaelic football, just a few miles down the road. At the time, it looked as though this was not going to happen for political reasons stated in Rule 42 of the GAA Constitution. In the end, the GAA voted to allow Croke Park to be used temporarily until 2008 for non-Gaelic sports such as rugby and soccer, while Lansdowne Road was redeveloped, and Ireland would play their home games in the 2007 Six Nations at the stadium, which ranks among the world's best.

Although Brian greatly admired the surroundings of

the Millennium Stadium, he knew that the Welsh crowd would give the home team a massive boost and this would be an intimidating place to play.

On the day, the squad made the short coach journey from the Hilton Hotel to the Millennium Stadium and Brian was struck by the sheer number of people out on the streets of Cardiff wearing red. Welsh rugby had never known a day quite like this, certainly not since Wales's heyday in the 1970s. This was going to be a massive test for his team.

The atmosphere inside the Millennium Stadium was no less intense. Brian felt the full force of a boisterous Welsh crowd as he led his men on to the pitch. The match that followed certainly lived up to its billing.

Ronan's early penalty kick gave Ireland the lead and Stephen Jones missed the chance to level the scores with a kick of his own a few minutes later. A drop goal from Gavin Henson brought the scores level.

Ireland had the better of the opening exchanges until the 16th minute when Wales scored a try in bizarre circumstances. Brian impressively turned over the Welsh ball and passed out to Ronan, who took rather too long to put the ball into touch, allowing Gethin Jenkins to charge it down, after which he kicked the ball ahead, patiently allowing it to fall over the line before placing himself on top of it. Hardly the sort of try people had got used to seeing in games of this standard, but the fact was it put Wales in front, leaving Ireland with it all to do.

Stephen Jones duly converted, before Gavin Henson put another three points on the board with a mammoth kick from inside his own half.

Brian didn't disappoint with his level of commitment in trying to get Ireland back into the game when he sent Denis Hickie on the charge with the ball, but Girvan Dempsey was held up on the line by a superb Stephen Jones tackle. However, a while later, Brian let his enthusiasm get the better of him when he came in at the side of a ruck, which resulted in Jones adding three more points to the Wales tally.

Ronan's kicking was as reliable as it had been for most of the tournament and his penalty narrowed the lead shortly before the break, but there was no hiding the enormous fight back Brian and the team had to mount in the second half.

Things went from bad to worse in the opening exchanges of the second half as two penalties from Jones extended the Wales lead to 26–6, and Ronan didn't make the task any easier by pushing one wide when they most needed him to be on form.

Anthony Foley had a decent chance to score but was forced into touch by Shane Williams. It was clear by the hour mark this wasn't going to be Ireland's day. A Kevin Morgan try sealed Ireland's fate and by now the scoreline was impossible to turn around with just 20 minutes left to play.

Wales became complacent allowing a close-range try by replacement Marcus Horan to bring the score to a respectable 32–20 with seven minutes left, making it a nervous finale for the Welsh fans. However, Wales held their nerve and the Grand Slam was in the bag, in what was one of the most memorable days in Welsh rugby history.

Brian was not as distraught as one might expect following the defeat. He was stoical and gracious, accepting that his team had been beaten by the better side on the day, and there were no excuses and certainly no English-style whingeing from him or any of the Irish camp. Brian said a sincere well done to his old friend Mike Ruddock at the captain's reception that night.

The following day, he and the rest of the squad headed for Kehoe's bar in Dublin for the traditional end-of-tournament wind-down. The purpose of this had become a sort of unofficial debrief and to make sure the players felt good about themselves and the state of Irish rugby for the rest of the season. If any of the players had been feeling downbeat following the Wales defeat, they had certainly snapped out of it by the Sunday night and this was to be an old-fashioned rugby gathering, the sort that had largely disappeared in the professional era, and it was time to have some fun and let themselves go at the end of a long, hard campaign.

Brian and some of the others headed out into Dublin

for a proper night out that lasted well into the early hours. Needless to say, Brian took the rest of the day off before returning to training with Leinster on the Tuesday. That night was to be the last time the Ireland squad would see each other and be on the same side for a number of months. The end of the Six Nations also marked the end of another era. The Ireland team manager Brian O'Brien was retiring after five years in the post. A quiet, unflappable yet canny operator, he was somebody who Brian O'Driscoll held in high regard and he was sorry to see him leave the setup.

The Six Nations campaign that promised so much yet ultimately led to disappointment was at an end. The first phase of the most important year of Brian's career was over. It was time to look to the challenges that he was going to face in the months ahead.

# CHAPTER 3

# THE GREATEST HONOUR, THE GREATEST CHALLENGE

On the following Wednesday morning, Brian was listening to the radio while having his breakfast when he heard an interview with Clive Woodward, who gave details of what he was looking for in a Lions captain. He used the exact same words he'd used to Brian at his home in Henley. Not a Martin Johnson clone, but somebody with his single-minded approach.

Brian knew that the interview was probably pre-recorded as Clive was away on holiday that week, but what could this mean? Was the captaincy in the bag? Or was Clive taking some time away to ponder his decision? Brian's heart began to race as his thoughts turned to the future and what this could all mean.

Within a day, he had snapped out of it and reassessed his priorities. He reminded himself that first and foremost it was a privilege to even be selected for a Lions squad and if picked to play he owed it to himself and the team to try to produce the best rugby of his life.

In the meantime, he had to focus on his responsibilities with Leinster but this was easier said than done. The Six Nations had completely dominated his life since Christmas and he had thought about little else day and night over the past three months. Now it was over and he felt a real sense of anti-climax. The adrenaline had gone from his body and all of a sudden every bump and knock he had experienced during the tournament had come back to haunt him. His body felt battered, bruised and exhausted, but he knew he couldn't sit back and relax for too long as Leinster's vital Heineken Cup match against Leicester was just around the corner and he had to be back in shape for that.

Most importantly, his hamstring wasn't quite right and he knew that it was important to give it time to heal if he was to be fully fit for the Leicester game, so he decided to sit out Leinster's Celtic League fixture the weekend before.

His relationship with model Glenda Gilson – of which there had been much gossip in the Irish press in the preceding months – was back on, but Brian was keen to keep things as low profile as possible. Comparisons had been made in the Irish press to Posh and Becks, but in reality nothing could have been further from the truth. Their relationship had been on and off a few times before and they certainly did not do much to court press attention, especially outside Ireland, where hardly anybody had heard of her. But the fact he was seeing such a glamorous woman inevitably meant their relationship would attract the attention of the press.

Yet there was an upside to the high profile Brian now enjoyed in Ireland. He had become something of a marketing dream in his home country, and now, more than ever, advertisers were keen to have him associated with their products. Second only to Roy Keane, he was Ireland's most marketable sportsman.

The Irish rugby press had noted that Brian would regularly be seen drinking from a bottle of Powerade, and argued that it was happening too often to be a coincidence. Then there was the golf club on the Wicklow–Wexford border that Brian had described as 'an amazing place'. He had just signed an exclusive sponsorship deal with the club. He said of it, 'When I visited [the club], I knew right away I had found what I was looking for; I can finish training and be on the first tee here in just over an hour.'

Observers depict Brian, who holds qualifications in sports management, as level-headed and financially savvy. In 2001, he set up a company to handle many of his commercial deals. His father, Frank, is a director of the company and advises his son on which offers to take. ODM Promotions made a profit of around €125,000 for the year ending 31 August 2003 and had retained profits of €188,000. But, by now, things had moved on considerably.

One Irish sports agent said that, if Brian was offered the Lions captaincy, he could charge whatever he liked. He said, 'For example, he's in such high demand to make personal appearances he can probably ask for around ?5,000 a day. He's in a take-it-or-leave-it position.'

Fintan Drury, chief executive of Drury Sports Management, tried to put Brian's earning power into perspective. He explained, 'Other than being a fantastic player, he's bright, articulate, young and has a good image. However, there's a very simple equation at work here – rugby players don't earn as much as footballers, there is a massive gap.'

Drury was blunt in comparing Brian's earning power with that of Roy Keane. He said, 'If Brian were to have as long a career as Roy Keane has had, regardless of what he is getting paid by his employers at the IRFU, he still wouldn't be in the same league. It doesn't matter how successful he proves to be with the Lions – Adidas is always going to be able to sell more pairs of boots with a football player.'

Another agent, who has experience in handling several Irish rugby players, backed up this view, saying, 'It's a

Mickey Mouse sport compared to soccer. Roy Keane makes more in one month than Brian O'Driscoll could possibly make in a year. Keane can get away with asking for £10,000 a day for personal appearances. In rugby that's just not on. You can't even really compare it to the likes of tennis or golf. Padraig Harrington probably makes several million a year in prize money alone.'

Times have certainly changed since rugby turned professional, but these accounts go a long way towards showing that the earning power of even the most glamorous and high profile of rugby players does not even come close to matching that of other sports. As the press attention surrounding his private life proves, Brian was, by now, much more than just a rugby player in his homeland – he was a celebrity in his own right. So, the fact that he does not have the financial clout of other sports stars from Ireland may come as something of a surprise, yet it is clear that Brian has benefited considerably from the professionalisation of rugby and his earning power is considerably higher than it would have been had he come along a decade earlier.

One down side the professional era had brought was the criticism he had to face for not turning out for Leinster in Celtic League matches as often as many traditionalists would have liked. On this occasion, he really did need to rest his hamstring and save himself for the Heineken Cup.

To this point in the season, he had played four Celtic

League games, six in the Heineken Cup, which require a similar standard of preparation to internationals, and eight Ireland matches, giving a total of 18 full-on games by the middle of March. In the old days, there would have been one international in the autumn and four games in the Five Nations, plus some far less demanding club games, and that would be about it. There is no comparison between the intensity of the two eras, and the physical demands placed on the modern players is undoubtedly more intense. On this basis, few would argue that leading players such as Brian should be preserved for the key games.

Since he was 'resting' that weekend, Brian decided to head on a night out with his mates in Dublin on Friday night. On the Saturday morning, he headed for brunch at a local café. While he was there, he received a voice message on his mobile from Clive Woodward, who was still on holiday somewhere in the Caribbean. Clive asked him to call back as soon as possible, but Brian had difficulty getting through to him. He tried again 15 minutes later. Still no luck.

Brian knew full well that this phone call would either make or break his hopes of being Lions captain. All this waiting to get through to Clive was torture.

It seemed like many hours, but in truth only about 20 minutes had passed when Clive's phone finally rang. They exchanged pleasantries for a few moments – it turned out Clive was in Barbados in the baking heat and had just come back from a morning swim. Then came the big news. Brian was formally offered captaincy of the Lions. Brian immediately accepted, and clenched his fist and punched the air for joy.

It took a minute or two to sink in. He recalled the meeting in Henley a few months earlier, but then in the past few weeks the press had bandied about other names and Clive was playing his cards very close to his chest. Brian needn't have worried. Clive had pretty much decided on the night of the Henley meeting that Brian had matured enough as a person and was now absolutely the right man to captain the Lions.

There was no time for wild celebrations as Clive immediately began talking about the hectic schedule that stood in front of him in the months ahead. First up was the big lunch on Monday, 11 April at the Hilton Hotel, Heathrow, for the management and captain. Brian would be expected to arrive on the Sunday night and the big announcement would be made live on Sky on the Monday afternoon.

Brian's attempt at humour fell flat: 'I'm not sure I will be able to fit that in,' he said.

There was a long pause at the other end. Clive seemed irritated.

Brian came back with: 'Well, of course I suppose I could try to clear the diary,' to try to show he was joking.

There was another long pause. Clive clearly didn't see the funny side and said, 'Well, it would be nice if you could find time to pop in, Brian.'

Hardly the best start to his tenure, but it was all soon forgotten. Brian was sworn to secrecy for the next two weeks until the official announcement was made. He was allowed to tell his parents, but that was about it.

During the course of the following week, Clive phoned Brian a number of times to discuss the tour. Brian was pleasantly surprised by the amount of input Clive was giving him regarding squad selection. Clive made it clear to him that he was the man leading the team and ultimately he had to be happy with the men he was leading out.

Brian had some very clear thoughts on the players he wanted to be included. The exception to this was the front row, about which he admits he knew very little, but there were a number of people on hand whose views he respects to make recommendations for him.

By the end of the week, he had put together a list of 53 players that had to be reduced to 44 by the following weekend. Thirty-five of these were definite, but there were still a few either/ors and there was plenty to play for in the week ahead for a number of players.

That Saturday was the day of Leinster's vital Heineken Cup game against Leicester Tigers at Lansdowne Road. Brian knew he could not underestimate the sheer power of the opposition who were going for their third Heineken Cup. In truth, Leinster took an almighty hammering that day as the Tigers became the first English side to win a Heineken Cup quarter-final away from home.

The Leinster defence did remarkably well to keep the score down to a respectable 29–13 but in truth they were never in the game, and had to settle for a late consolation try from Shane Horgan.

One positive Brian could take from the game was the impressive display put in from Geordan Murphy who was now in with a serious shout of making the Lions squad. The papers were massively critical of Leinster's performance but there was no point in dwelling on it. It was over and Brian had no choice but to look forward to the Lions tour.

# CHAPTER 4

# LEADING BY EXAMPLE

As captain, he was eager to set an example to the rest of the squad so he threw out all the junk food he had in his kitchen and stocked up on fresh fruit and veg, as well as chicken and fish cutlets. He knew that it would be boring rabbit food all the way for the next few months, with very few beers and heavy nights out with the lads. He owed it to himself and the team to be in the peak of physical fitness and to prepare properly for the tour.

Brian began the week well and stuck rigidly to his new regime. But his plans were interrupted on the Wednesday when it was announced that Declan Kidney had resigned as Leinster coach and was taking over at arch rivals Munster. Declan cited family reasons for the move, but his side's thrashing the previous weekend made his position at Leinster less secure. Brian had heard a rumour the previous week that Declan had applied for the vacancy at Munster and was sure he'd take it if offered.

It's fair to say that Brian's relationship with Declan had never been particularly close or easy. They first worked together when Brian played in the side that won the under-19 World Cup in France in 1998. At the time, they worked well together, with Declan teaching Brian never to go out on to the pitch feeling inferior to his opponent – a lesson he has never forgotten. That was probably the high point in their relationship, and at Leinster things had never been as good between them.

The previous week, Declan had wanted to talk to Brian about the way ahead for the rest of the season. Knowing something was up, Brian cut him short, telling him it was a pointless exercise because he knew full well he wasn't going to be there. Mentally, Declan had not made the break from Leinster and even offered to stay there for the remainder of the season, but that was never going to be an option.

Some of the other members of the squad were certainly not sorry to see him go. He had just finished a round of contract negotiations and told several prominent members of the team their contracts were not being renewed, and Brian tended to side with the players over Declan over this.

Brian could not hide his frustration with the way things had developed at Leinster under Declan's tenure – he did not believe his overall game had progressed as he would have liked.

He knew what he would like to see in Declan's successor at Leinster – a technically brilliant coach who had new ideas and innovations he wanted to put in place. He also knew that such coaches wouldn't come cheap and that he had to detach himself from the mess at Leinster because of his commitments with the Lions.

It was now less than a week until Brian would be unveiled as Lions captain at the big press conference in London. Brian spent the weekend doing some quiet sightseeing with Glenda in London. Clive phoned Brian and told him the make-up of the final squad. Brian was delighted with Clive's choice; every 50-50 decision had gone the way he'd hoped and he was comforted to know that he and Clive thought alike on matters of team selection.

They both knew the importance of persevering with Jonny Wilkinson, allowing him extra time to recover from his injury. The Kiwis would have loved them to announce this early on that Jonny was injured and wouldn't be on the plane, so they agreed it would be better to do exactly what the Kiwis didn't want them to do. The same went for Mike Tindall and Phil Vickery, both of whom were extremely doubtful but would keep the opposition guessing until the very last minute.

Brian checked into the Hilton Hotel in Heathrow under the name Marcus Jansa, who was presumably friends with Brendan O'Donovan and Graham Delaney. He spent the night before the big day watching Tiger Woods winning the US Masters golf after a nail-biting play-off.

On the day itself, he was not allowed out of his room until midday to keep the growing press entourage guessing for as long as possible. He was then smuggled via the service lift to the press-conference room where he was kept waiting behind the curtain before being unveiled.

Clive had not really prepared Brian for the occasion. There was to be no autocue or script. He wanted it to come from the heart. Brian had to overcome his shyness because the truth was that once in New Zealand there would be press conferences most days and he simply had to get used to this intense level of media interest.

Brian played it safe at the press conference. He knew that every word he said was being taken down by a large number of journalists and that there were many thousands of people listening live on television. This was not a time for any of his lame attempts at humour.

Instead, he just went through the motions, saying what an honour it was, how moved and emotional it was to be selected as captain, and how hard it had been not telling anyone other than his parents about it those past few weeks.

Inevitably, the journalists were more interested in the apparent absence of Jonny than in Brian being named captain, and this press conference proved relatively easy for him. The only question that really came his way was when he was asked about his memories of previous Lions tours. Aside from the tour of four years previously, his memories were virtually nil and, when asked what he remembered from the previous Lions tour to New Zealand in 1993, all he could say was, 'I was much more interested in Mark Hughes and Manchester United in those days'.

After the press conference was over, they split up for one-on-one interviews that gave Brian the chance to say all the things that had been playing on his mind over the last few weeks.

At mid-afternoon, Brian took a flight back to Dublin and organised what he intended to be a small gathering for close family and friends. This soon erupted into a wild party with at least 40 people turning up at his house, which included no fewer than six members of the Leinster squad who had been selected for the tour.

Denis Hickie, Shane Horgan and Gordon D'Arcy had been on edge for at least a week. They knew they were borderline selections and the build-up to this day had been a nervous one for them. Brian had known for several days that their seat on the plane was secure but he was sworn to secrecy and had to watch them suffer, unable to say a word.

Shane Byrne and Malcolm O'Kelly would be joining them, as would Ronan O'Gara, a controversial selection but one Brian was very keen on, believing him to be the best fly-half available. Yes, there had been the occasional very bad performance with the boot, but he had generally been in good form over the previous four years, though he would face stiff competition from Stephen Jones to make the first XV.

The night started with some serious talk about how Brian saw the tour progressing, but before long they had all had plenty to drink and the lads, continuing the celebrations, headed to Flannery's pub – a haunt often frequented by nurses who had just come off shift. After that, they went on to a club and let themselves go before a daily disciplined routine had to set in.

The following weekend, Brian was spurred on by the news that Jonny had played a successful 50 minutes for Newcastle on the Friday night and was looking good for the tour. Brian played in Leinster's Celtic League win over Glasgow, although he was disappointed with the way his team fell away in the second half and blamed himself for not fully concentrating. However, considering all the upheaval at Leinster, it wasn't a bad performance by the boys.

## Leading by Example

On the Sunday, Brian travelled to the Vale of Glamorgan hotel near Cardiff for a two-day Lions get-together, exactly a month before they were due to fly to New Zealand. Waiting for Brian at the hotel was a large brown parcel. He opened it to find a Blackburn Rovers shirt signed by Mark Hughes, who had heard Brian's reference to him at the press conference and took the opportunity to write Brian a personal note wishing him all the best for the tour. 'Sparky' was Brian's all-time sporting hero and he felt greatly touched by this gesture; the shirt now takes pride of place on Brian's wall at home.

The purpose of this exercise was just to spend a bit of time together as a squad. They had been used to knocking lumps out of each other for the past four years, now they were on the same side and had to get to know each other as rugby players and as people.

In the evening, Brian and a few others had a great laugh filming the tour trailer for Sky. Brian spent half an hour roaring like a lion in front of the cameras, but couldn't help falling about laughing every time he tried to look remotely menacing. The finished article saw their heads turned into those of lions, thanks to some help from computer animation, and certainly made for an impressive advert.

Training wasn't a massive priority during this gathering, though Brian did put in several weight sessions, but gave his legs a well-earned rest. The most important aspect of this gathering was the briefing given by Clive and tour manager Bill Beaumont, which included a lot of emotive language about the Lions.

Representatives from each of the four nations, Martin Corry, Gordon Bulloch, Gareth Thomas and Paul O'Connell, were asked to explain what the Lions tour meant to them. Then it was Brian's turn to give his speech. For once, he knew exactly what he wanted to say and there was a very important message he wanted to convey to his players.

He pointed out that the only previous Lions tours people really remembered were the tours of 1971, 1974 and 1997, which were all winning tours for the Lions. Hardly anyone mentioned the 2001 tour, and that was only four years ago. Other tours such as those in 1993, 1983 and 1977 are almost entirely forgotten, because the Lions were defeated. Brian made it clear to the squad that it was up to them to make this tour one people would be taking about in fifty and hundred years' time.

Brian also made it clear that, after a night's celebrating on the day of the squad selection, he had knuckled down to training like never before in his life. He was leading by example, and expected every single member of the squad to follow suit.

Brian then talked about what he and Clive had discussed in Henley at the start of the year. This tour had

74

to be fun. They would be together as a squad for seven weeks. This would be the only time in their lives they would play together as a squad, and it was important they had fun and enjoyed each other's company.

He told them to enjoy New Zealand, a country like Ireland in many respects with its relaxed pace of life, village feel and warm welcome. He pointed out that the New Zealand players were far more humble and friendly than their Southern Hemisphere counterparts. Warriors on the pitch, but gentlemen off it. The New Zealand public were rugby-mad and would give the players a warm welcome if they walked into a hotel or a bar, and the players should enjoy mixing with the ordinary people. There were also to be some old-fashioned school and hospital visits, something that hadn't happened too often in recent years.

Brian got his message across well. It would be a tough tour rugby-wise, but ultimately playing for the Lions is the pinnacle of any player's career and it was an experience to cherish and enjoy, especially in such a beautiful country as New Zealand.

There were a number of other 'getting to know you' exercises during the get-together, which included one member of the squad interviewing another in depth. Brian got paired off with Welshman Shane Williams, who he didn't know all that well, and it proved to be an interesting exercise. Brian learned that Shane wasn't some wonder-kid and had been something of a late developer. This meant he had to work hard for everything he had earned in the game.

This was music to Brian's ears. He knew instantly that Shane was a grafter and was exactly what was needed for the battle that lay ahead. Brian knew from the interview that if Shane was feeling a bit down on tour he responded better to the carrot than the stick. He also discovered that Shane was mad on motorbikes and that was his main interest outside rugby.

Then the roles were reversed and it was Shane's turn to interview Brian. Shane asked whether Brian had any embarrassing moments and if he had any regrets. Brian had one good story that answered both of those questions.

A few years earlier, Brian had done some advertisements for men's pants that resulted in some horrendous posters of him posing in his underwear. They were unflattering to say the least and Brian had kept a low profile for some months afterwards.

Later on, Clive and the rest of the management team quit the room and left the players on their own to come up with their own Code of Conduct and outline their tour objectives. Brian allowed Lawrence Dallaglio, a veteran of the successful '97 tour, to head the discussion. Obviously, there would be disappointed individuals who would not be selected for the Test side and they had to agree now the best way to deal with this. They also discussed the best way to support players who were having a bad day at the office.

At the end of the meeting, Lawrence came over to Brian and gave his take on the matter. As a veteran of two Lions tours, and the holder of a World Cup winners' medal, Brian took what he said very seriously.

Lawrence made it clear to Brian that there could be no bad days at the office on this tour. These matches were among the most important any of them would ever play and they had to give 100 per cent all the time. This was the philosophy they had to live by and this was the message they had to get across to the rest of the squad. It was as simple as that.

Clive returned to the room after an hour and the squad presented their findings to him. He agreed to give them every important thing they wanted. The tour charter was agreed and it would be printed into a booklet and given to each player the following month.

There were some amusing team-building exercises during the get-together that, on the surface, look silly but which Brian actually found a very effective way of getting to know members of the squad better and understand how they work as a team. Firstly, there was a mosaic exercise with a Lions theme which saw all the national flags and emblems split into 100 squares. Each team had to paint a few of those squares, which meant co-ordinating with the teams in charge of the squares bordering yours. It was a good laugh and they looked like primary-school children at the end, covered from head to toe in paint, but it achieved an important objective.

There was more fun after the team dinner when the squad was split into nine teams and each team was expected to perform cabaret. This kind of extrovert behaviour really didn't come easily to Brian and he just had to make the best of it. Ben Kay's celebrity impersonations were undoubtedly the highlight of the cabaret exercise, with a small number of others just about managing not to make complete idiots of themselves.

But again, there was a far more serious wider purpose to the task. A squad of players, who didn't really know each other that well beforehand, had come together and learned a bit about each other and learned to work together as a team. Of course, there is no substitute for training and playing together, so Brian was delighted when a pre-tour game against Argentina was set up, but this gathering had done a great deal to boost team spirit and morale.

Brian returned to Dublin at the end of the get-together, and it was only a matter of days before he discovered there was a nasty flipside to his elevated level of fame.

He had been living very happily at 'number 35' and had found he could go about his business quite easily without too much hassle. He lived surprisingly modestly for a man of his stature and was happy just being an ordinary bloke when he was among his local community. However, his profile had undoubtedly rocketed in the last few months, especially in the few weeks since he was named Lions captain. Things were about to change, and Brian was about to get a very rude awakening and see the other side of life as a famous sports star.

Brian returned from the get-together in Wales to find youngsters literally camped out in his garden waiting for him. Across the road, he could see several photographers hiding. He had no front gate and no privacy. This was becoming a problem and potential threat to his safety. He knew the time was right to move.

He had his eye on a property in Dublin's Herbert Road, but he couldn't afford it just yet. Brian had become something of a property bore just recently, and would flick to the property pages in the local paper even before checking the rugby results.

Brian was also still slightly distracted by the Leinster situation. They had finished a disappointing third in the Celtic League, way behind the Ospreys and Munster, and Brian met with some senior members of the squad to discuss the best way forward. Brian held the view that Leinster urgently needed a specialist coach who could take their individual games forward as well as put an overall game plan into practice.

In the days and weeks that followed, Brian found himself obliged to do more interviews than he had ever done before. As Ireland captain, he was now well used to having to do a number of interviews per day. Now he was captain of the Lions, and this meant the intensity and quantity of the interviews would only increase. But Brian stuck to his well-rehearsed routine. He remained firmly on message and made sure he said the same thing in every interview. He knew from past experience that an attempt at trying to be humorous could easily be taken out of context and this was certainly not the time to be starting a war of words with anyone.

The key point Brian tried to get across in every interview was that all 44 players getting on the plane on 25 May stood a realistic chance of getting in the Test side. The same could not be said of the 2001 tour. There was competition for places. Even a fit Jonny Wilkinson could not take his place in the team for granted with Stephen Jones in such superb form.

Brian made it clear in these interviews that he did not even dare take his own place in the team for granted. Yes, he was captain, and, by right, that should mean that he was an automatic choice. Yet he knew that he had to prove every day that he was worthy of his place as there were players who would more than hold their own at centre. He knew he had to lead by example, to play the best rugby of his life and encourage those around him to do the same.

Brian stated that, for him, a Lions tour to New

Zealand held as much gravitas as playing in a World Cup final. He also repeatedly praised Sir Clive Woodward and the coaching setup, and said the preparation to date could not have been better.

At the end of April, Brian took a break from the Lions build-up by playing for Leinster in their Celtic Cup quarter-final clash against Glasgow. The tournament might not have been at the top of Brian's priority list at the beginning of the season, but Leinster had crashed and burned in all other competitions and capturing this piece of silverware would give a much-needed morale boost to the squad following Declan Kidney's departure.

Leinster won the game but the performance was hardly convincing. They had moments of skilful brilliance but these were more than outweighed by shoddy defending that almost allowed Glasgow to steal the game.

Unsurprisingly, it was the in-form Brian who was at the heart of Leinster's most impressive move of the match when he charged into the defence and threw a back-flip pass into space, knowing full well Gordon D'Arcy was running into it. Gordon then passed out to Girvan Dempsey to score a well-rehearsed, perfectly executed try.

The following week Brian declared that enough was enough and there would be no more press interviews for the time being. He decided that there was enough physical and psychological preparation to be done in the short time that remained before the plane left and he felt he had been more than generous with the time he had given the press and had easily fulfilled his obligations as captain.

In one of his last interviews, Paul Ackford in the *Sunday Telegraph* drew attention to the size of Brian's arse. Paul was taken aback by how stocky Brian was when he saw him in the flesh. The truth was that the game had changed a great deal in the last few years and Brian was a good example of how world-class centres in the future would be built.

Brian received some encouraging news from Clive when he was told that Jonny had come through a full 80 minutes for Newcastle, scoring six goals and setting up a try against London Irish. It's hard to see how the news could have been more encouraging, but Clive wanted to see him play another 80 minutes before making his final decision.

Brian began to focus purely on the rugby, and there was nothing quite like a match against Munster for focusing Brian's attentions. This was the Celtic Cup semi-final, and Brian did not underestimate the importance of this game.

Yes, it was undoubtedly important for Leinster to receive a lift after the season they'd had. Yet it was also important that Brian and all of the other Lions tour players who took to the pitch had some competitive match practice with the days ticking by until the plane left.

The match was a typical niggly encounter between the two sides. Kiwi Dave Holwell was sent off for Leinster over a petty incident with just five minutes to play. The game was tight and this left Leinster feeling unbalanced and allowed an Anthony Foley try to steal the game for Munster in the final minute.

It was a disappointing and frustrating end to a pretty miserable season for Leinster. The season promised so much yet everything fell away, although there was no denying the part off-the-field problems at the club contributed towards the disappointment.

Brian knew there wasn't time to dwell on it and he simply had to focus on the Lions from now on. That same evening Clive phoned Brian to tell him that Jonny had come through another 80 minutes and was fit to go on tour. This gave Brian's mood a massive lift. He firmly believed that Jonny was the best fly-half in the world and his inclusion in the squad would rumble the All Blacks. He also knew that Stephen Jones was in the form of his life and Jonny would have to stay on his toes to keep his place in the team. Inevitably, there were a few injury worries in the squad but this news gave a massive boost to Brian and lifted the morale of the whole squad.

Clive was less happy with his former employers at the RFU over their attitude towards England coaches and staff involved with the Lions tour. They had each received a letter asking them to log any time over 15 minutes they spent on Lions business before their contracts officially began on 17 May. Clive was understandably outraged at the pettiness of it but soon decided not to waste his time fighting a battle when the squad needed to be focused on other things. Brian saw this for the comical squabble it was, and decided not to waste his time elbowing in on something so silly.

The following day, Brian's problems were put firmly into perspective when he discovered that the Leinster team doctor had suffered an unbearable tragedy on the Saturday. Jim McShane's three-year-old son Teddy had been killed in a drowning accident. Brian was very fond of Jim and his wife Dolores and was greatly saddened by the tragedy. At the funeral just two days later at Dun Laoghaire, Brian was moved to tears by the sight of the little white coffin being carried down the aisle at the beginning of the service.

The whole Leinster squad attended the service and it reminded every one of them that there were far worse things in life than losing a game of rugby.

They had been planning a squad night out to say farewell to a number of players who were moving on. Victor Costello was retiring, while David Holwell was returning to New Zealand. Meanwhile, Shane Jennings and Leo Cullen were moving to Leicester. The original plan was to meet in Kiely's in Donnybrook, but following the tragedy nobody was in the mood for celebrating. Instead, they had a few quiet pints before agreeing to meet up again under happier circumstances.

The rest of the week was a rare lull in Brian's hectic schedule. It was very much the case of being the calm before the storm. He kept his body in shape but didn't over-train; instead, he used the week to tie up some loose ends.

He took some time out to read the sack loads of good-luck cards and letters he had received, which included a letter wishing him well from Taoiseach Bertie Ahern. Other notable well-wishers included former Lions captain Ronnie Dawson, which Brian greatly appreciated.

The squad were going to get together at the familiar surroundings of the Vale of Glamorgan hotel in the days before the flight to New Zealand, and the time had come for Brian to say goodbye to friends and family. It wasn't so much a case of saying 'goodbye' to those closest to him – most of them would be taking a trip out to New Zealand to watch him play at some point – but it certainly was a case of saying goodbye to his home, to his familiar surroundings and to Dublin, a place he would not see again for another two months. From now on, he would be living out of a suitcase.

Brian checked into the hotel early on the Monday morning, before making the two-hour trip to London for a TAG photoshoot, then back to Cardiff for another shoot with Gillette and then back to the Vale for some more snaps for Adidas. The hectic schedule of that first day away from home helped Brian forget the nervous feelings he had been experiencing for the last few days. That evening, he bumped into Jonny – who was looking in trim shape and ready for battle to commence – in the hotel lobby.

The following day was far more boring, with most of it spent on administrative matters such as filling in insurance forms and autographing piles of memorabilia. During the course of the day, most of the rest of the squad arrived at the hotel and checked in. The one notable exception was Iain Balshaw who was forced to withdraw from the tour with a quadricep injury.

Brian felt a great deal of sympathy for Iain's predicament and it served as a firm reminder to him and the rest of the squad that they were all just one bad tackle away from being out of the tour themselves. An in-form Mark Cueto took Iain's place in the squad, which came as some consolation to Brian who had seen the rich try-scoring form he had been in for Sale during the season.

It so happened that the Manchester United team were staying in the same hotel that week as they were playing in the FA Cup final at the Millennium Stadium that weekend. This allowed Brian an opportunity to talk properly to one of his all-time heroes, their captain Roy Keane.

Known for his no-nonsense captaincy and blunt way of getting his point across, Roy had some firm advice for Brian. He told him to be his own man, to look after himself and make sure he was on top of his game. Brian was already doing exactly this, but hearing it from someone who had been there, done that and got the T-shirt, as well as being a fellow Irishman, certainly meant a lot. The principles of captaincy in both sports are much the same and this chat went a long way towards boosting Brian's confidence in his own ability.

On the Saturday, the whole Lions squad headed to the Millennium Stadium to watch Manchester United play Arsenal. As a massive United fan, this was a dream come true for Brian who had not had the time to watch his beloved team play for 18 months. He had also never been to an FA Cup final before, so this was a big day for him, and a chance to take his mind off the upcoming tour for a while.

The whole squad had VIP tickets but Brian insisted on turning up in United colours and certainly wore his heart on his sleeve during the game.

The match went to penalties following a goalless, but entertaining 90 minutes. Arsenal ultimately won the shoot-out, which left Brian in a grumpy mood as he had to endure a great deal of taunting from Llanelli coach

Gareth Jenkins, a fanatical Gooner. Nevertheless, Brian enjoyed the opportunity to switch off and let others do the hard work for a change.

After dinner that evening, Brian and the others not taking part in the warm-up game against Argentina on the Monday were given permission by Clive to go into Cardiff for a night out. It would be their last opportunity to have a proper drink for at least the next two weeks.

They headed off into town in their Range Rover, complete with minders who had previously served in the SAS. They had got a few miles down the road when their vehicle suddenly ground to a halt. The minders leaped out instantly to protect the players from any kind of sabotage, though there was nothing to worry about.

After using their military experience to identify the problem, the SAS veterans discovered that the problem was, rather embarrassingly, that they had run out of petrol! Another standby vehicle was provided and they were soon on their way again.

Cardiff was still buzzing from Wales's spectacular Grand Slam victory and Brian and the lads enjoyed mixing with the Welsh public in the clubs and bars that evening. Inevitably, as the evening wore on and the drink began to set in, a small number of people approached Brian and the others looking for a fight. Fortunately, the minders were never too far away and there were times during the evening when their presence was greatly appreciated.

# CHAPTER 5

# DOWN TO
# BUSINESS

The following day, Brian had a bit of time to himself as the emphasis switched to those playing against Argentina. At a bit of a loose end, he decided to have a listen to the iPod every member of the squad had been given. On it was a favourite tune selected by every member of the touring party. Many of the Irish players chose U2. Will Greenwood was a big Neil Diamond fan. Alastair Campbell, the former New Labour spin-doctor and press secretary to Tony Blair, was part of the tour party to work on the PR side of things. His selection for the iPod was Abba's 'The Winner Takes It All'. He had told Brian it was the first song he'd heard on the radio when he woke up the morning after the 1997 general election.

The team selection for the warm-up match against Argentina was always going to pose difficulties. Clive had decided some weeks before that it would not be a good idea to let Brian play in the game as to lose your squad captain to injury under those circumstances would obviously be considered a disaster.

Gareth Thomas was an absentee as he was playing in the Heineken Cup final, and fellow Welshman Stephen Jones had club commitments in France. The five Sale players were needed for the Challenge Cup final, and Neil Back was serving a two-week suspension for punching Joe Worsley. Others would also be sitting out as they were recovering from knocks, but the big news was that Jonny would be taking part. It was felt he could do with playing a competitive 80 minutes against a world-class side given the length of his latest injury lay-off.

The instructions to the team for this game were simple – it was not to be treated as some kind of meaningless warm-up game. The priority was to win the game, and put in a good performance, in that order. Sections of the press were ridiculing the fixture as pointless, and a bit of a joke. Others said the fixture was reckless risk-taking, which could lead to key players picking up injuries with just a matter of days to go until the plane left.

Brian and Clive didn't see it like that. Only a fool would fail to acknowledge that Argentina were now a force to be reckoned with in world rugby and they would offer the Lions a highly competitive match.

A number of automatic picks were being rested, which allowed a degree of experimentation. This meant those lucky enough had to put in a good performance. Those who could expect to play in the Test side had to confirm to Clive and Brian that they were in top form, and those players considered fringe members of the squad had to make the most of this opportunity to state their case for Test selection.

So Brian took his place in the stand to watch the match. The performance was somewhat disjointed and a number of basic errors allowed the Pumas to dictate the game. A try from Ollie Smith kept the Lions in the match but the star of the game was Jonny who kicked an injury-time penalty to secure a 25–25 draw. This game was certainly no warm-up for Jonny – it was a statement of intent on his part. He proved to the world that he was back and that he meant business in the tour ahead. Brian didn't become too distracted with the fact the Lions didn't manage to win and instead expressed delight at Jonny's return to his very best.

Shortly after the match, Clive revealed some disappointing news to the rest of the squad. Jason Robinson would not be flying out with them later in the week as he felt he needed to spend some time with his wife, who was pregnant and the situation was causing him some anxiety. Gareth Thomas and Stephen Jones would also be joining up late, as they couldn't be released from club commitments in France. Michael Owen would be flying out but would be returning home just a week later to attend the birth of his child. Clive's decision to take a huge squad was now beginning to look like a very smart move.

On the day the squad flew out to New Zealand, Brian received some welcome news from Leinster. Michael Cheika had been appointed Director of Rugby while David Knox would be joining as backs coach. This news was exactly what Brian wanted to hear. Knox becoming backs coach especially pleased him, as he was a man Brian knew a fair bit about and greatly respected. He was confident that the new Australian coaches at Leinster would help take his game forward.

And so Brian took to the skies in a flight lasting more than 24 hours. He boarded wearing his Lions blazer and full suit, though soon changed into a T-shirt and tracksuit bottoms once on board. The whole tour party was large enough to require two planes since there weren't enough business-class seats on board for everybody. Brian stopped over briefly in Singapore prior to flying on to Sydney to meet up with the rest of the squad before they embarked on the final leg to Auckland together.

Upon arriving in Auckland, he was greeted by around

150 hardcore Lions supporters who had already made the long trip, along with one New Zealand supporter who challenged him with his unique version of the haka.

Brian and the rest of the squad decided it would be best to try to stay awake for as long as possible to adjust to the New Zealand time and so headed for a few beers and a stroll along the harbour front after they'd checked into the hotel.

The following day, Brian met up with some members of the New Zealand squad who were involved with promotional work with Adidas. Brian especially enjoyed the chance to spend some time with his friend (at the time) Tana Umaga, who is regarded by those who know him as a complete gentleman off the pitch, softly spoken and very charming, despite his fierce, warrior-like persona during battle.

Brian knew that, away from the field, relations between the two squads were going to be very good. The New Zealand players were exactly as he expected them to be – warriors on the pitch but humble and unassuming off it. He knew from then on that the tour was going to be good-natured and there was going to be no unpleasant war of words between the two groups of players.

Later that same day, Brian spent some social time with Jonny. The conversation that followed was to have a profound effect on him. Jonny began to tell him how his life had changed since England's World Cup win two years earlier. Jonny was very much the star of the team and had become rugby's answer to David Beckham.

Like Brian, Jonny had never been an extrovert off the pitch and was not comfortable with some of the aspects fame had brought him. He now needed full-time security guards and was mobbed everywhere he went. He was forced to spend most of his spare time indoors and simple things like walking down the streets near his home had become extremely difficult. The long injury lay-off had given him time to think and he had decided that once this Lions tour was over he was going to take measures to try to lead a more normal lifestyle.

This chat made Brian consider just how lucky he really was. Yes, there had been problems recently with his own security, hence his need to move home, but generally he was allowed to go about his business without massive difficulty and the way ordinary people were with him rarely gave cause for concern. Yet he knew that now he was Lions captain this could all change. Until now, his fame was largely confined to Ireland. Now, he would be as well known in Great Britain and this could have consequences when he made his regular journeys there. Would it be practical for him to go for nights out in British cities from now on? Would he be able to go shopping in London with his girlfriend without being mobbed? He needn't have worried, but at the time these were very real concerns for him.

## Down to Business

The next day, the whole squad attended the official Maori welcoming ceremony, which was a plane ride away at Rotorua. They were greeted at the airport by thousands of rugby fans, before being taken by coach to the venue, which, due to the heavy rain, had to be moved indoors.

They were told on the way that they would have to respond to the Maori warriors' song with one of their own. Brian knew that Matt Stevens had a great voice and asked him if he fancied the challenge. To his credit, Matt knew all the words to 'Bread of Heaven' and responded in style.

Once inside the hall, Brian was greeted by a Maori elder who gave him a warm welcome. Brian went on to make a polite speech in which he said that, while his team were there to win, they were also in New Zealand to make friends and to enjoy everything the country had to offer. The tour manager, Bill Beaumont, then accepted the challenge laid down to him from the spectacularly dressed Maori warrior, complete with spear. Brian thoroughly enjoyed this ceremony, which was the first of many experiences the squad would have of New Zealand's rich culture.

One aspect of the preparation Brian did not enjoy was being coached for the many press conferences and interviews he would have to undertake as Lions captain. He believed he was already doing well in interviews,

95

generally playing it safe, remembering to repeat the same party line in all interviews, no matter how repetitive it had become. As Ireland captain, he thought he had gained enough experience to be considered pretty good at this.

Alastair Campbell had been brought on the tour party to deal with PR issues and to make sure everybody was singing from the same hymn sheet. While Brian liked Alastair as a person and enjoyed his humour and passion for sport, he did not like some of the advice he was given.

Alastair had come from the world of politics where he had gained a controversial reputation in his role as Tony Blair's press secretary. In Brian's mind, politics and rugby were worlds apart. He understood that politics was essentially a murky and cynical world where a few words taken out of context could be twisted to mean something very different, whereas rugby was an entirely different matter. The game was generally played in a gentlemanly manner and there was a strong moral code among players that was generally adhered to. Compare the response a rugby referee gets from the players to that received by a Premier League football referee. The game is played in a gentlemanly spirit and differences can usually be resolved over a pint.

Brian felt he already knew how to behave in interviews and didn't always feel Alistair's attempts to manage them were necessary. From time to time, he had strong views and said things that needed to be said, and felt it important that he would continue to be allowed to express himself honestly and frankly during the tour.

The first training session brought home to Brian the extent to which the squad's every move would be followed by the public and media. The training session was watched by around 2,000 supporters. It was intended as an Open Day so there was no great disruption caused by the crowd, although it did provide a fair few laughs.

Sky commentator Miles Harrison was providing commentary for the crowd and the players had to do an official run-on. Being the captain, Brian led the party and sprinted on to the field, only for the rest of the party to stitch him up by staying put in the tunnel, much to the amusement of the crowd. However, a few moments later Brian got revenge thanks to the wonders of modern technology.

A promotional video was being played on the big screen, which, it turned out, wasn't quite big enough, as it cut off the first two letters of everybody's names. For Brian, this was no big deal, as he simply became 'ian O'Driscoll'. Things weren't quite so straightforward for Steve Thompson and Gethin Jenkins, who picked up rather unfortunate nicknames for the rest of the tour.

The one serious issue that arose as a result of this

session was that Clive and the coaches decided that the group training sessions were too shambolic and that there would be no more such sessions for the rest of the tour. It was a decision Brian didn't completely agree with as he felt there were benefits to be had from everybody training together, but on this occasion he had to bow to Clive's decision.

Attention soon turned to the first match of the tour where the opponents would be Bay of Plenty, who had finished third in the National Provincial Championship (NPC) the previous year. Club rugby in New Zealand is intensely competitive, and Brian knew there would be no easy games against club sides. Every match would be a battle. And so it proved.

At half-time, the scores were level at 17–17 as the opposition gave everything they had. The Lions managed to run in three tries in the second half, although there could have been a fourth courtesy of Brian but he messed things up. Mark Cueto was unmarked on the outside and was calling for the ball, but Brian chose to pass to Josh Lewsey on the inside who couldn't do much with it. Mark was furious and started shouting at Brian, before realising it was the captain he was speaking to and apologised profusely. He needn't have worried. Brian knew he had messed up and deserved everything Mark was throwing at him. The Lions eventually won the game 34–20.

Brian's main concern following the game was Lawrence, who had been taken to hospital with a broken ankle. The injury was severe and threatened to end his career. Lawrence was a larger-than-life character, and an experienced old head who Brian greatly appreciated having around. His loss was a huge one for the team, but also a major psychological blow to Brian, and certainly took the gloss off an impressive second-half performance.

After the game, the players headed off for a few quiet drinks. There was little point in trying to sleep as the adrenaline was still pumping. It wasn't a heavy night out, but it was a good chance to unwind after the baptism of fire they had just experienced.

Brian used the following day to relax – there was no way a heavy training session would benefit him at all. He watched the New Zealand version of *Strictly Come Dancing* in his hotel room. Former All Black hooker Norman Hewitt was the star of the show, getting perfect marks from the judges for his *paso doble*, which included a haka in the middle. Later that day came the more sombre task of welcoming Lawrence back following his operation. His tour was over, but he wouldn't be able to fly home for another 10 days and offered to help Brian out with the preparations, which he greatly appreciated.

Simon Easterby was being flown out as replacement for Lawrence, and within a matter of days the squad would be at full strength. Stephen Jones and Simon Shaw had just arrived and had joined up, too. Gareth Thomas would be joining up shortly as Toulouse had just been knocked out of the French Championship, and Jason Robinson would be arriving at around the same time.

Halfway through the following week, Brian was hit by a nasty dose of food poisoning after he had made the mistake of eating scallops, his favourite seafood, the previous evening. He tried going to training but soon had to throw in the towel and was violently sick. Within 24 hours, he had lost four kilos but he was soon over the worst.

Later that week, he flew up to New Plymouth for the first of the community days. Brian spent an hour watching a group of 16-year-old boys taking part in a full-on contact session. Brian told them that what they were doing was deeply impressive, but it was equally as important to brush up on basic ball skills, which they didn't seem to put as much emphasis on.

Brian was asked to do some babysitting for one of the mums who was more interested in watching the training session. Ever the gentleman, Brian held the newborn girl on his lap. In New Zealand, they get the children keen on rugby from a very young age, and the baby, who can't have been more than a few months old, was already kitted out in All Blacks gear as she slept in Brian's arms.

He returned to the hotel to prepare the squad for that

evening's game against Taranaki. Brian was going to sit out the game because a huge test against New Zealand Maori was only a few days away, and he needed to rest his shoulder, because the old injury had come back to haunt him once more.

Brian watched the game from the stand with his cousin Jenny. The Lions were captained by Martin Corry who led the side to a 36–14 victory against strong opposition, which included two superb tries from Geordan Murphy. A number of fringe players had certainly staked their claim for a place in the Test team. Brian flew straight back to Auckland after the game to prepare for the match against Maori.

Brian chose to take things easy the following day, aware that any heavy training sessions could aggravate his shoulder problem and could force him to miss the game. Instead, he spent part of the day in the casino, where he made a small profit, before going with Shane Horgan for a haircut. The woman cutting Brian's hair claimed she used to work in Dublin and knew his favourite bars.

The day was very much the calm before the storm. The match ahead had been billed as the 'Fourth Test' and there was undoubtedly going to be a Test match atmosphere inside the ground come the day. Thirty-five per cent of all rugby players in New Zealand were eligible to represent Maori, and Brian was well aware that they were a proud race and would be taking this game very seriously.

Those players that might or might not be eligible to play for the Maori have their credentials examined by the Maori kaumatua, who traces the players' genealogy. The process is famously complicated, one notorious example being that of Christian Cullen, who it was discovered was 1/64th Maori and therefore eligible to play.

Later that evening, Brian watched a rugby programme on TV1, which had no fewer than six studio guests. Former All Black wing Stu Wilson was one of them, and he refused to join in with some of the harsh criticism the Lions had faced in the press the past few days from the likes of Jon Mitchell. Instead, Stu said that he had been impressed with what he had seen so far and expected some fiercely competitive games ahead.

Following the rugby came the weather forecast, presented by the gaffe-prone Brendan Horan, who described the weather as: 'Bloody ugly, just like the Lions front row.' This sort of thing only spurred Brian on even more.

The day before the match Brian did some light training, though he remained cautious because of the shoulder problem. In the evening, he watched the highlights of New Zealand's warm-up game against Fiji on television. The All Blacks thrashed Fiji 91–0, but Brian still picked up on weaknesses, particularly with regards to their tackling. This was, nevertheless, the first time the All Blacks had played together since the previous November and Brian knew that the team that had thrashed France the previous year would soon get it together again and the challenge that lay ahead would still be incredibly tough.

The match against Maori was watched by a sell-out crowd of 30,000 at the Waikato Stadium. The atmosphere was exactly as Brian had anticipated, and it was clear to everyone involved this was a full Test in all but name.

The opening exchanges were physical with neither side giving an inch. Stephen Jones opened the scoring with a penalty but Maori soon brought the scores level. The pressure on the Lions was relentless until eventually Martyn Williams handed the Maori the lead when he deliberately slowed the ball down, giving Hill a kickable penalty.

Stephen Jones brought the scores level but soon sustained a nasty injury after colliding with a Maori shoulder. He left the field with blood pouring from his face and was replaced by Ronan, but he was soon patched up and was able to come back on for the remainder of the game. Andrew Sheridan was then given 10 minutes in the bin for a punch on Luke McAllister but the resulting penalty was not converted, making the scores six a piece at half-time.

The second half saw Maori turn on the class and kick three penalties early on. This was followed by a try from Leon MacDonald which was converted. Several Maori penalties were added soon after and the Lions became increasingly frustrated and sloppy.

With the game lost, Brian restored some credibility by scoring a try following a rolling maul, which was converted by an in-form Jones. The captain had led by example, but it was only ever going to make the score look more respectable. Brian had captained the first Lions side ever to lose to Maori.

Once back in the dressing room, Ian McGeechan tried to lift the team's spirits following the historic defeat. He compared that night to the first game of the 1997 tour when the 'Test' team were defeated by a very average Northern Transvaal side. Apart from a few moments of brilliance from Jeremy Guscott, the Lions played incredibly poorly. Ian told the players that for about half an hour after the game they were feeling down, but then the true spirit of the Lions came through and they decided that from then on they would destroy every South African team that came their way. Just four days later John Bentley scored a breathtaking try and the tour was back on course.

Clive reinforced this point by telling his players that this defeat would make them, not break them, and that, between now and the next game, they would concentrate on the good, and work on the bad. Brian simply told his men to ignore whatever criticism the papers threw at them over the coming days. It was what went on within the squad that mattered. Everything else was irrelevant.

Despite scoring a try that night, Brian felt he had put in a poor performance and asked Clive if he could play in the Wednesday game against Wellington to make up for it. Clive agreed, and named a strong team for that game, which included the likes of Jason Robinson and Gareth Thomas, who were making their tour debuts. Clive also decided that this would be a good time to unleash Jonny, who would be making his Lions debut in New Zealand on the day.

The squad flew on to Christchurch in preparation for the Wellington match. They trained on the grounds of Christchurch School, one of the best rugby schools in the country. Brian had seen many hakas by now and felt he had become immune to its effect, but nothing could have prepared him for what he saw at the end of that training session.

It was a longstanding tradition for the school to issue the haka when Lions tour parties used the ground. Brian stood in awe as around 600 boys, some as old as 18, lined the quadrangle to perform the haka. He had never seen anything like it in his life. It was a truly breathtaking experience for him, and one that would stay with him.

Brian hadn't spent much time reading the papers over the previous few days. It was inevitable that his team were being criticised left, right and centre by the press following the defeat. However, he had found out about one story that annoyed him more than any other.

Several papers had reported that there had been a training-ground bust-up between Gordon Bulloch and John Hayes that had left Gordon needing a few stitches. Brian firmly denied there had been any such bust-up, and that Gordon's injury had been caused by a boot when they were practising their rucking. For him, this was a story out of nothing, a bit like the day before the squad was announced when one national paper declared that Matt Dawson had been excluded, when in fact he knew full well there was a plane ticket with his name on it.

The Wellington match took place before a crowd of 34,000 at a ground affectionately known as the Cake Tin. The opposition was strong – they were missing their All Blacks stars but they would still provide formidable opposition. This time the Lions performance was far more impressive as tries from Welsh duo Gethin Jenkins and Gareth Thomas helped secure victory. It wasn't perfect and there were still plenty of things to iron out in training, but it gave a much-needed morale boost to Brian and the rest of the squad.

The following day, the papers were not talking about

the result; instead, they focused on Jonny's tour debut and what this would mean for the team selection for the upcoming Test. He was brought on after an hour as replacement for Gavin Henson, switching Jonny to inside centre alongside Brian and bringing Stephen Jones on as fly-half. Clive had considered moving Jonny as far back as the initial meet-up in Cardiff, and he was using this opportunity to experiment and see how it worked out.

However, this got the papers and, more importantly, the All Blacks guessing as to what they were really up to. Were they trying out variations just to give Stephen Jones more time? Nobody except the Lions themselves knew for sure.

In the end, the decision was taken to play Jonny at 12, thereby allowing the Welsh Grand Slam half-backs to remain together. The only person who would be disappointed by this arrangement would be Gavin Henson.

Gavin's tour was far from over but he made little attempt to hide his disappointment at being omitted from the Test team. Shortly after the tour, he published a diary in which he slated several members of the Lions squad and questioned some of the tactics employed and preparation for matches. There had been some bad blood between Gavin and Brian that had spilled over into the public arena around this time.

The fall-out began during the Wales–Ireland Grand Slam decider earlier that year. Gavin had claimed that Brian swore at him and called him 'cocky' during the game. He also claimed that Brian had tried to 'jackal' him, a term players use to mean stealing the ball from your opponent on the ground.

Gavin's criticisms didn't end there. He claimed that Brian had pulled his perfectly styled hair during the game and also tried to gouge his eye for good measure, before saying, 'How do you like that?'

Once Gavin's book was published shortly after the tour, he gave his reasons for not liking Brian, in as strong terms as he would be allowed to use. Essentially, it seemed that there was a simple clash of personalities between them. Gavin objected to Brian's in-your-face, confrontational manner on the pitch, whereas he preferred to keep quiet and let his play do the talking.

They were also poles apart away from the pitch. Gavin and his girlfriend, the singer Charlotte Church, had become a celebrity couple in their own right, especially in Wales. They liked to be seen together in public, courted media attention and enjoyed living the celebrity lifestyle. Gavin was also gaining something of a reputation for his appearance. His hair always looked as though he had styled it with meticulous attention to detail, and he was often ridiculed for shaving his legs.

In sharp contrast, Brian's approach was more that of

the traditional rugby player. Yes, he kept himself in the peak of physical fitness and was a role model for the professional era, but it would be unthinkable for Brian to lead a 'showbiz' lifestyle. He preferred a few beers in the company of close friends to attending film premieres, and, although he and Glenda could easily have become a showbiz couple if they'd wanted to, Brian preferred things to be low key and to keep his private life private.

Once the tour was over and Gavin's book was published, Brian said in an interview that Gavin had criticised certain players in the book but had never criticised them to their faces. The book caused much controversy and also saw Gavin say negative things about members of the Welsh Grand Slam squad, which led to a souring of relations between himself, his team-mates and the Welsh Rugby Union. Since then, Gavin's game has been in decline and he has never fully recovered from this episode.

Preparation for the first Test began in earnest and Clive decided that work had to be done to improve line-outs. The problem seemed to be that the codes were too easy for the opposition to crack so they were deliberately made more complicated in the days leading up to the match.

Clive gave the players the impression that the All Blacks were spying on them and using underhand techniques to find out their game plan. It was equally as plausible that he was doing it to strengthen squad unity and make them think and act more cohesively, but either way, security had been stepped up significantly.

Brian found out the sheer professionalism and scale of the security operation while chatting to one of the regular security men who had been around him since the start of the tour. He told him that since the start of the week there had been three or four extra security men put in place. There was no point in Brian trying to find them, because they were so professional and so well hidden.

There were obvious security implications in having such a large number of world-class rugby players in one place. They were a high-profile target for terrorists so nothing could be left to chance. But, with Clive telling his men that the All Blacks were trying to spy on them, the role of the security men took on a whole new purpose.

From now on, nothing was left to chance. There would no longer be opportunities for waiters and other hotel staff to listen in on their conversations. Scribbled notes would no longer be thrown away in wastepaper baskets, as it would be all too easy for someone to pick them out of the bin and pass on vital information to the All Blacks. Every time the squad moved to a new hotel, every room would be swept for bugs and other listening devices.

If he was being serious, it wouldn't be the first time something like this had happened on a Lions tour. There had been speculation four years previously that South Africa had learned their line-out calls and the Lions had paid a heavy price for this in the third Test. Martin Johnson, one of the best in the world in a line-out, lost several balls he would normally be expected to grab with ease. There could be no repeat of that this time around.

All meetings would now take place in the 'War Room' as opposed to the Team Room. That would be the place where game plans, line-out calls and all notes would be kept. It was to be guarded 24 hours a day and no paperwork was to be taken from there under any circumstances.

For Brian, the consequence of this was that he became more withdrawn and less willing to interact with the public than usual. He was still willing to sign autographs when out and about in the streets, but he became a very private person in his hotel and didn't appreciate strangers coming up to his door for trivial reasons. This atmosphere of suspicion, combined with the fact that the first Test was now only a week away, resulted in considerable changes in Brian's personality. He became very focused, his whole life was consumed by the Lions. Other things did not matter and he did not allow himself to get distracted by them.

Even on his days off, he was thinking about nothing other than the Lions. If he went for a walk, it would be by himself. He got some bad publicity in the local press after withdrawing from some community events, but deep down he knew this was the lesser of two evils.

Those who have met Brian in passing or at a function nearly always agree that he is quiet and affable, and pretty generous with his time. At this moment in time, that was not the case, and it was better to just allow him to shut himself away from outside distractions. The usual Brian O'Driscoll simply did not exist until after the first Test.

This change in mood had consequences for his relationship with Glenda. Things seemed to be going well between them, and Glenda had planned to come out to see Brian during the fortnight, but he was now dead set against the idea. The last thing he wanted to do now was go for quiet meals in restaurants or take walks with her around some of the spectacular scenery that surrounded the hotel.

Sleeping next to her at night would also pose problems. He was prone to waking up, full of adrenaline and needing to go for short walks to clear his head. Other members of the squad, especially those who were married, seemed to love having their partners around during this crucial time. Perhaps for those who were married things were different. They would know one another's faults far better and knew when to give each other space. Brian's relationship with Glenda was still in its early days and there was no way he was going to jeopardise things by revealing this darker side to his personality at this stage.

His parents were due to fly out shortly to watch him play, although he preferred not to meet up with them either just then. His relationship with them had always been fairly close and he knew that allowing them to see him when he was like this could not be a good thing.

Brian was by no means the first rugby player to behave like this when away on tour. He had found out that former All Black Colin Meads would never even phone his then fiancée Verna when away on tour, following an incident when Colin, who was clearly in a similar frame of mind to Brian, had a blazing row with her while away in Australia. This brought out an uncharacteristic side to him she had not seen before, and from that point onwards they agreed to communicate twice a week, by letter. He had obviously done something right because they have now been married for more than 40 years.

It was clear that Brian would have some making up to do once the tour was over, but that was something to think about later. For the time being, only one thing mattered.

# CHAPTER 6

# THE CHANCE OF A LIFETIME

Brian travelled down to Dunedin to watch the second string take on Otago. The side, captained by Gordon Bulloch, put in an impressive display as they secured a 30–19 victory. There were two major talking points that came from the game.

The first was when Otago captain Craig Newby accused the Lions of 'cheating like buggery' at the breakdown. Coach Ian McGeechan shrugged off Newby's comments in the post-match press conference, telling journalists that they must have been doing something right to get him to make such an outburst.

Secondly, there was Ryan Jones's breathtaking debut at number eight, earning him the man of the match award. He had only been a part of the squad for a few days, having just flown in from Wales's tour of Canada where he was taking the place of the injured Simon Taylor. He scored one try after Shane Williams did the groundwork, then later on he returned the favour by setting up Shane following an almighty charge at Otago.

The following day's papers highlighted Ryan's performance as well as that of Simon Easterby, and several journalists pondered why it was that in such a close-knit squad the star performers were those who joined the party late. This was a fair question, but Clive put it down to them being extremely determined to impress when their chance came. The truth was that these two were now not far off being selected for the Test team.

The day had arrived when Clive would announce which players would make up the Test side, and which would be left out. To put it politely, those who were left out would make up the squad to play Southland. The whole squad were gathered for the big announcement. Aside from Gavin's absence, which Brian had known about for several days, there were a number of other very able players who had done little wrong, but were nevertheless destined to take on Southland rather than the All Blacks – Geordan Murphy and Charlie Hodgson to name but two.

Clive told the disappointed men that their contribution

in training in the run-up to the big day was vital. They were well-intentioned words, but they came as little consolation to the men who had come so near, and yet so far, to making the Test team.

The Southland squad were then asked to leave the room, leaving just the 23 members of the Test squad and the coaches. The make-up of the squad provided no real surprises. Shane Horgan was chosen over Shane Williams for a place on the bench, which was a very tight call, but beyond that the press chose to focus on Gavin's omission and Jonny's switch to number 12.

Clive then went on to talk through the game plan, aided by diagrams he had drawn on the board. The chosen few looked on in a dazed silence, many of them still coming to terms with their inclusion in the side, while eager to absorb what Clive was saying at the same time.

At the end of the talk, Brian retired to his room and watched the final of the New Zealand version of *Strictly Come Dancing* on television. Brian watched as Norm Hewitt proved once again that there was far more to him than just his skills as a rugby player. Norm put in a brilliant performance on the dance floor, and Brian sent in a few text votes to prop up his chances. Sure enough, the New Zealand public agreed with Brian and Norm was crowned champion.

At midweek, Brian watched from the stands as the

second string just about managed to scrape a win against Southland. It was by far the Lions' worst performance all tour, and was not the kind of preparation the squad needed for the first Test, which was now only a matter of days away.

There were some highly talented players in the Lions team that took to the field that night, and Brian expected far more from them. Many critics believed that the players who took to the field were playing as individuals, rather than as a team unit. They were inevitably extremely disappointed at not being part of the Test squad, and felt they had a point to prove to earn their place for the second Test. As a result, team play went out of the window and they all suffered because of it.

Clive had told Brian that Wales's Australian backs coach, Scott Johnson, was flying out to act as an observer for the Lions. Scott had caused massive controversy the previous autumn when, during the build-up to Wales's game against the All Blacks in the Millennium Stadium, he referred to New Zealand as 'just a poxy little island in the Pacific'. The proud nation of New Zealand was about to take its revenge on Scott.

Upon arriving at the airport, Scott showed his passport to the girl at the desk and, after she typed his number into the computer, she looked a little concerned and went to fetch her supervisor. Scott stood around for a long time, and got increasingly worried about what might be happening. Then, a huge man wandered over with his passport in his hand, before making a show of inspecting it in minute detail.

After a lengthy delay, he said, 'Ah, Mr Johnson, we have been looking forward to your arrival for some time. A thousand welcomes to our poxy little island in the Pacific. I do hope your stay with us isn't too awful.'

Scott was for once lost for words.

The build-up to the big day was gathering pace, and Brian joined the squad for the big team announcement opposite the hotel that evening, which was broadcast live on New Zealand television. It was a glitzy occasion, complete with a big screen and musical fanfare as they entered. However, what was meant to be a well-rehearsed formal occasion soon turned into a bit of a farce.

Enough seats had been set out for the squad, but one of the journalists decided it would be funny to take a few of them away to try to encourage a scrap between players for the seats that remained. To make sure all formality went out of the event, Paul O'Connell couldn't resist the opportunity to pull Alastair Campbell's tracksuit bottoms down, turning a revered and feared spin-doctor into a figure of fun.

The day before the big game, Brian tested out the pitch at the Jade Stadium, aware that wet weather, possibly even snow, would be on the way the following day. Later that evening, he spent time in the company of his sisters. Still very much in his withdrawn, focused mindset, these were the only people in the world he could bear to spend time with at the moment. They knew all about his mood swings and were willing to make allowances for them, considering the highly pressured circumstances.

Brian went to bed that night knowing he could not be more ready. His preparation had been perfect. He was in the peak of physical fitness, and had never felt as sharp as this. His mental preparation had been spot on and he knew what he wanted and what he expected from his team-mates. His recurring shoulder injury was holding up well, and there was no way that was going to stop him from taking to the field. Even the dreaded hamstring that messed up his Six Nations campaign was holding up well now. He would be able to run at full speed, confident that it would not let him down. He was in the form of his life, and the tour couldn't have come at a better time. There were no excuses, Brian was ready for battle and he slept well that night, confident he could handle whatever the All Blacks threw at him.

The day Brian had waited six months for had arrived, and Brian led his Lions team out on to the field in the intimidating, yet electric atmosphere of the Jade Stadium. After the anthems had been played, it was time to face the haka. Brian and Clive had discussed at length the most appropriate way to accept the challenge. They agreed that the last thing they should try to do was upset their opponents. This was, after all, a longstanding tradition and they were ultimately guests in their country. Of course, there was also a chance that if they upset the All Blacks at this stage it might spur them on even more and increase their determination to beat the Lions, which is the last thing they wanted to do.

Brian recalled a conversation he'd had with a Maori elder at their official welcoming a few weeks before, who outlined the most appropriate and respectful way to accept the challenge, and decided to follow his advice on the night.

Brian, as warrior chief, stepped forward to directly oppose their chief, Tana Umaga, accompanied by the youngest member of the team, Dwayne Peel. The rest of the team spread across the pitch, completely motionless. It was one of those moments that everyone involved would never forget. Tana led the haka with extra enthusiasm and it was very clear that Tana the gentleman was left behind in the dressing room and Tana the ruthless warrior had taken to the field. He put everything into it and tried to look as intimidating as possible as Brian stared straight into his eyes. Yes, it was steeped in ancient tradition, but it was also the perfect curtain-raiser for the battle that would follow. When the haka was finished, Brian remembered what the Maori elder had said and leaned forward while still maintaining eye contact, clutched a piece of grass and threw it to the wind. In the days that followed, the New Zealand media claimed that the Lions had insulted their hosts with the manner in which they had accepted the haka. Clearly, Brian and Clive knew more about the history of the haka than most of their critics did. They had done their homework perfectly. Brian had chatted to a Maori elder, and he and Clive had kept in contact with him via email to make sure they got it exactly right. Brian couldn't win. They could not have done more to get it right and it was clear that he was right and they were wrong.

With the formalities over, it was time for the rugby to begin. Within a matter of seconds, Brian tackled Leon McDonald, but Leon laid the ball back well, and Jerry Collins formed a protective bridge. Brian got back on his feet and started leaning on Jerry to try to get him to crash into Justin Marshall and spoil their possession.

Brian became aware of their hooker Keven Mealamu trying to pick him up by the left leg, which was completely illegal, but he might still have considered the ruck to be live. Brian was considerably stronger than Keven and managed to get the better of him. Tana had driven through the ruck, and moved left as Marshall cleared the ball. With the ball now well away from them, Tana turned back to Brian, grabbed his right leg and lifted him up. Keven helped Tana lift Brian, before turning him upside down.

ar is born: Brian celebrates a hard-fought victory over France, and an awe-inspiring
vidual display of skill.

*© PA Photos*

Relaxing on the British and Irish Lions tour of Australia.

*Above*: Brian enjoys a round of golf in Perth.

*Below*: When in Australia do as the Aussies do – trying his hand at surfing with Dan Luger.

...n breaks away to score the Lions' third try in the first test against Australia at the ...ba (*above*) and celebrates the 29-13 victory (*below*). © *PA Photos*

*Above*: Brian walks off the pitch dejected after the Lions lost 35-14 in the second test

*Below*: Captain Martin Johnson is consoled by coach Graham Henry after losing the final test and the series. Rumours of an unhappy camp were rife, and Brian and Graham did not enjoy an especially warm relationship. © *PA Ph*

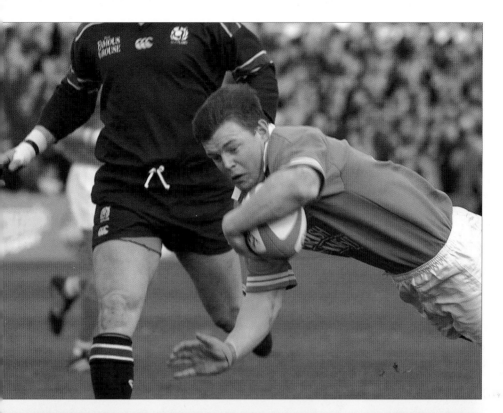

*ve*: Back to his best! After something of a blip in form Brian returned in
*tacular fashion in the 43-22 victory over Scotland in the 2002 Six Nations.

*w*: Made captain for the 2003 Six Nations, Brian led Ireland to four
*ecutive victories, including this one over France at Landsdowne Road.    © *PA Photos*

*Above*: 'Drico' goes over the line against Australia in the 2003 World Cup pool match. Ireland came agonisingly close but lost 16-15, though they still qualified for the quarter finals.

*Below*: Despite his best 'Superman' impression, Brian couldn't stop Ireland crashing out of the tournament against France.

© PA P

...ve: The captains get together prior to the 2004 Six Nations (*from left – right*): ...es' Colin Charvis, Brian, England's Lawrence Dallaglio, Italy's Andrea di Rossi, ...land's Gordon Bullock and France's Olivier Brouzet.

...w left: Brian runs at the England back line as Ireland beat the World Champions 19-12.

...w right: Brian wins his 50th cap in the Triple Crown decider against Scotland.

Celebrating winning the Triple Crown with coach Eddie O'Sullivan.

Brian was about to crash to the ground, and his priority was to break his fall. He knew if he landed on his head he would break his neck and face a life in a wheelchair. He stretched out his right arm just in time and hit the ground hard. He was in agonising pain, and quickly realised he had a dislocated shoulder. He tried shouting out to touch judge Andrew Cole, who was still standing by the ruck, but he had no voice at all. Maybe he had been winded, maybe the shock had made it impossible for him to speak. Meanwhile, play had moved to the far side of the pitch and Brian was left the forgotten man.

The incident occurred close to the Lions fans and they knew exactly what had happened. Eventually, play was stopped on the other side of the field when the Lions halted the All Blacks close to the line. Brian's pain was only increasing and it wasn't long before physio Phil Pask called for the cart and diagnosed a dislocated shoulder.

Many rugby watchers described Tana's spear tackle as the worst they had ever seen. It was illegal, reckless and the ball was well away from them by the time Tana dropped Brian to the ground, so there can be no possible excuse for it. Yet it was four months before the authorities decided to punish him.

At first, they accepted his explanation that it was 'accidental' but all those months later some amateur footage shot by a well-placed spectator showed the sheer dangerousness of the tackle. The fall-out from the incident was enormous.

It's clear that Tana didn't acknowledge Brian as he was being taken off the pitch that night, in fact, the only All Black to enquire after him was Justin Marshall. Some time afterwards, Tana phoned Brian, and a hostile exchange took place.

The details of what was said remained a secret until late 2007. Brian left the details out in his official Tour Diary book and his ghost writer was forced to tone down some of the more severe criticisms aimed at Tana, at the insistence of a sportswear company who sponsor both men. In his book, Brian says that the two had agreed not to divulge the details of their conversation.

Tana however claims that Brian was angry that he had not called him sooner to discuss the matter. He also says that Brian was furious that he hadn't gone over to see how he was, and accused him of being involved in a lot of off-the-ball incidents.

In his own book, Tana accuses Brian of being a 'sook', a New Zealand slang word meaning 'cry baby'. He says that he never went out to injure Brian and that, in the heat of battle, rugby players do occasionally sustain serious injuries. It appears likely that Brian was absolutely furious with every aspect of the tackle, and wasn't willing to dismiss it as just one of those things.

Few would disagree that the tackle was extremely dangerous, reckless and completely unnecessary, but the incident also ended what had until then been a good friendship between Brian and Tana. The incident certainly left a sour taste in the mouth and the remainder of the tour would not be played in the spirit of goodwill and friendship that had existed until that point.

Phil and Brian's cousin, Gary, tried to push the shoulder back into place but they couldn't. The cart that took Brian off the pitch was also completely inappropriate, as Brian felt every bump on the grass. An old-fashioned stretcher would have been better. It didn't help that Brian was paraded the long way around the ground before reaching the medical room. Brian has since said that the journey around the ground as he lay there, in agony and sweating profusely despite it being freezing cold, was the most embarrassing experience of his life.

When they finally arrived in the medical room, they were greeted by a scene of chaos. A spectator in the stand had been taken ill and the supply of morphine had been taken to help him. Sadly, the spectator subsequently died, which helped Brian put his own set of circumstances into perspective when he found out about it later on.

With no morphine available, Brian was lifted on to the table and the stadium nurse started to cut his Lions shirt off. Brian was now in excruciating pain, by far the worst of his life. A medic started using laughing gas on him to ease the pain, but Brian didn't take kindly to them forcing it down his throat. He pushed it away and asked them to just hold it above his mouth, which made things slightly better.

Incredibly, the nurse had the nerve to ask Brian if she could have his Lions shirt. Brian couldn't believe what he was hearing. He tried to use some very bad language but couldn't get the words out. The nurse persisted, saying she had two children and they would love to have it. She had no chance. The shirt was Brian's only artefact from the tour and he wouldn't part with it for the world. What else did he have left?

His father had fought his way through security and reached his son, who understood what Brian was fretting about. To Brian's eternal relief, the shirt was now in safe hands. After what seemed like an eternity, but what was probably no more than a few minutes, the medic found some more morphine and injected it into Brian's arm. Instead of giving it a few minutes to kick in, the medic immediately started trying to push the shoulder back into place. Brian was screaming in agony, he had never known pain like this before and just wanted it all to end.

From the corner of his eye, Brian could see Richard Hill coming into the room. His knee trouble had come back and he was out of the game, too, but was immediately taken to another room as Brian's screaming would have been hugely unpleasant to have to listen to. Eventually, his shoulder clicked back in. It was very painful, but Brian was relieved that it was firmly back in its socket.

Brian was then taken to the hospital, where the X-ray revealed no break, which came as a huge relief. The morphine was starting to kick in by now, so Brian can recall very little of his time in hospital. After a few hours, he returned to the hotel to meet up with his team-mates.

The match itself had been a disaster for the Lions, and the whole game had been played in a bad spirit following the tackle that was to end Brian's participation in the match and, inevitably, the tour. The All Blacks took the lead through a Daniel Carter penalty, which was followed by another soon after.

The first try came courtesy of Ali Williams after some clumsy work in the line-out from the Lions. Things went from bad to worse after the break when a stunning try from Sitiveni Sivivatu added to the misery. The only consolation came in the form of a Jonny Wilkinson penalty, but the final score was 21–3, which, if anything, flattered the Lions.

Back at the hotel, the atmosphere was as grim as Brian had ever known after a big game. The players were obviously down after the defeat, but they were outraged at what had happened to Brian. Every member of the team shared his view that he had been the victim of a malicious and dangerous tackle, and this was not just one of those hard but fair tackles that sometimes happen in a competitive game of rugby.

Later on, Brian met up with his family. Twenty-four hours previously, he didn't want them anywhere near him as he remained totally focused on the task that lay ahead. Now, though, he was only too pleased to see them. His family had always been a massive source of comfort and support for him, and now he needed them more than ever.

They sat in the corner of the hotel restaurant, saying very little. Brian's sister, Jules, was especially upset and had clearly been crying, although she made a good effort not to appear upset in front of him. At one point, the girls left the table, leaving Brian and his father alone together. Brian had never seen him as angry as this. His normally quiet and composed father was outraged at the tackle that had ruined his son's tour, shattering months of hard work and sacrifice in the process. It wasn't long before the girls returned, and he immediately calmed down to his usual self once again.

Brian knew full well that he wouldn't be able to sleep that night, so there was no rush to leave the table. At about 2am, he received news that the South African citing commissioner, Willem Venter, had refused to cite the two All Blacks involved in the tackle. This would have meant taking a proper look at the incident and interviewing all those closest to it. Incredibly, Mr Venter was intending to fly home in just a matter of hours. Brian was stunned by the extraordinary attitude the official was showing.

That said, Brian needn't have been so surprised. The precedents for bringing New Zealand players to justice on home soil weren't favourable. Two years previously, Ali Williams had been cited but cleared of stamping on the head of Josh Lewsey, an incident which left the England player with stitches and a badly bruised face.

Despite it being the middle of the night, Brian was inundated with requests for media interviews. He decided that he would release a statement. As Alastair Campbell had long since gone to bed, he did it on his own, and gave a full and frank account of what had happened from his point of view. The statement was completely blunt and spin-free. He was angry, and he didn't care who knew it. He had suffered a grave injustice at the hands of two of the world's toughest and most feared rugby players, and in the hours that followed the authorities didn't do anything to bring the men to justice.

He finally went to bed at around 4am, but he couldn't sleep. The whole episode just kept going round and round in his head. On the Sunday morning, Clive gave a press conference, as he had done on every other Sunday morning, for the benefit of Sunday-newspaper journalists in the UK. Even now, Brian wasn't going to let Alastair in on the act and reinforced everything he had said the night before.

Later that day, Brian was outraged by an interview he saw with All Blacks coach Graham Henry. He had played under Henry on the previous Lions tour when he was their coach and was hurt by his comments. In a nutshell, Henry brushed off the incident, but said that Brian was a good bloke and it was disappointing if his tour was over.

In the days that followed, Brian was outraged by the attitude taken by almost every New Zealand paper, with the exception of the *Herald*, which gave a fairer assessment. All other papers unquestioningly swallowed the line of the New Zealand camp, and didn't even entertain the possibility that Tana and Keven had been massively in the wrong. On television, the incident dominated every news bulletin. One of the channels managed to interview Andrew Cole, who had already flown back to Australia. He said that he didn't remember coming on to the pitch or ordering the players to put Brian down. After that, Cole clammed up in front of the camera when challenged and told the interviewer that he shouldn't really say anything. Incidentally, this was the same Andrew Cole who would be refereeing the second Test the coming Saturday.

Within a few days, Brian received the news that he would need a pinning operation to make sure the ligaments tightened properly so that the injury would not recur. It was already becoming clear that he was likely to miss the autumn internationals, which did little to lift his still very black mood.

As the week progressed, events did little to dissipate Brian's anger. Graham Henry stuck to his guns and said that Tana had apologised after the game, whereas in reality he had done no such thing. Someone from the New Zealand Rugby Union had been in touch asking for Brian's mobile number, which didn't impress him much. The hotel where the All Blacks were staying was only down the road, and it really wouldn't have taken much trouble for Tana, or even Keven, to pop over for a few minutes.

The All Blacks' spin machine proved more than a match for Alastair Campbell as they started briefing journalists that Henry had apologised on Tana's behalf, although anyone who had heard him speak during the press conferences knew his words fell well short of a proper apology. Their camp also accused the Lions of spinning the incident to make it appear more serious than it really was.

Brian was furious with Henry by this stage. He had worked with him four years previously but had never really warmed to him as a person. Yet he was still upset that Henry didn't have the grace to be more open about what had happened and accept that two of his players had been in the wrong.

On the Tuesday, the midweek team took on second-division side Palmerston North and won by a record margin of 109–6, with several players earning a place in the Test squad, including Shane Williams who scored five tries in the game. Brian watched from the stand and greatly appreciated the support being shown to him from the Lions crowd, who sported T-shirts bearing slogans such as: 'Keven Mealamu, Tana Umaga... all innocent. Yeah, right.'

This was the day that saw Brian's spirits begin to lift. He had a long chat with his father, who said that it was time to reflect on the fact that he was in one piece and to be thankful that he did not break his neck. In the evening, Brian received a text from his old friend Donal O'Flynn.

Donal had been a fine player in his own right and had made his mark at Belvedere College. When he was 17, he broke his neck, which left him quadriplegic. The text read: 'Both of us have many things in common. Same birthdays, both stunners, both great rugby players! And we have both taken personal setbacks with honour and dignity. Despite your recent hurt you remain a living Lion legend, Donal O'Flynn.'

After reading that message, the world didn't seem such

a bad place after all, and Brian knew he had plenty to be grateful for. Yes, there had been an enormous injustice and he would continue to fight to put that right, but there was little point in letting it dominate his mind for every minute of every day. It was time to move on, and to start plotting his comeback.

# CHAPTER 7

# MOVING ON

Despite being injured, Brian was not going to fly home immediately. He still had a great deal to offer as non-playing captain, and would be on hand to support the rest of the squad in the important challenges that lay ahead.

There were other obligations to fulfil, some of which Brian really wasn't in the mood for. One such instance was an official reception at the Parliament building in Wellington where Brian was booked in for a photo shoot with Tana. He decided it wouldn't be a good idea to turn up. He knew the media would be after photos of the two men shaking hands, and, since they hadn't even spoken at this stage, he decided it was inappropriate to proceed with this stunt.

Later that same night, Tana phoned Brian and the now infamous heated exchange took place. Despite his obvious anger during the call, Brian did not allow himself to be overcome with fury for too long, remembering that he had made a promise to himself to draw a line under the episode.

Glenda was due to fly out to join Brian at any time. Despite his having been hostile to having her around when he was part of the playing squad, she now couldn't arrive soon enough. Having his family around him those past few days had been a source of enormous comfort and support, and having Glenda around would make him feel far happier for the remainder of the tour.

He began to reflect upon his attitude in the lead-up to that first Test. Yes, he had been right to remain focused and determined to play the best rugby of his life, but shutting out those closest to him was perhaps not the best idea he'd ever had. He had now realised just how much he valued Glenda and his family, and knew that in future he'd have to strike a more sensible balance.

Glenda had respected his decision not to have her join him in New Zealand, but he now realised that she meant too much to him to just shut her out when an important match was approaching. After all, there were many members of the squad who loved nothing more than having their wives and children around them during the build-up to big games, and Brian now thought that maybe he had something to learn from their approach.

With time on his hands until Glenda arrived, Brian decided to go for a few beers with some of the New Zealand players who would not be taking part in the upcoming Test, including Conrad Smith, Doug Howlett and James Ryan. He enjoyed spending the evening in their company, and especially enjoyed talking to Conrad, who he found to be exceptionally bright and discovered he was training to be a lawyer.

The following day, Glenda finally arrived, which helped brighten Brian's mood. She could tell how disappointed Brian was with the way things had panned out but said all the right things. He seemed relaxed as they joined his family for a meal that night and he felt as though he could spend the time that remained on tour enjoying New Zealand and spending some valuable time with Glenda.

On the morning of the second Test, the papers were still talking about the incident, even though it was no longer dominating Brian's thoughts. He read a piece by Colin Meads, which summed up exactly what he was thinking. Colin said, 'Tana should have been around the Lions team hotel on Saturday night, Sunday night at the latest, with a crate of beer. It might have been frosty to start, but the thaw would have soon started. There is a lot of merit in the old ways.'

Brian couldn't have put it better himself. He was used

to settling on-the-field disputes over a few beers; it was the way he had always done things. This incident was an extreme example, but Brian freely admitted that, if Tana had behaved in the right way in the days that followed, he would soon have let it drop.

There was a series decider to be played that night, and Brian took his seat in the Westpac Stadium to watch as the Lions attempted to make amends for the previous week's disaster and level the series.

The Lions got off to a perfect start when new captain Gareth Thomas spotted a gap to score a superb try early on. Jonny was never going to miss the conversion, but a minute later he missed a golden opportunity to extend the lead further when his penalty kick hit the post.

However, it wasn't long before the hosts turned on the class through two cleanly taken penalties by an in-form Dan Carter, who went on to engineer a marvellous try for Tana, shrugging off Gavin Henson before charging 50 yards down the pitch to finish off the manoeuvre.

Jonny cut the gap with his first penalty eight minutes later but straight from the restart the Lions conceded a penalty and Carter restored the home side's lead. It wasn't long before the All Blacks scored their second spectacular try of the evening. After winning a scrum five yards out from the Lions line, they spun the ball across the width of the field allowing Sitiveni Sivivatu to score.

At half-time, the score was a respectable 21–13 but it

*ove*: In action for his club Leinster in the 2005 Heineken Cup quarter final.

*ove*: The greatest honour and the greatest challenge; Brian with Lions coach Clive odward after being named as captain for the tour of New Zealand. *© PA Photos*

*Above*: At the official opening ceremony in Rotorua.

*Below left*: Facing up to the haka with Dwayne Peel at the start of the first test.

*Below right*: Brian's tour is cruelly brought to an end within seconds of it beginning in earnest, the victim of a controversial spear tackle by Tana Umaga and Keven Mealam

*ve left*: Tana Umaga faces the press for the first time since the tackle on Brian, essing his innocence.

*ve right*: Clive Woodward makes his feelings on the tackle clear to the mbled press.

© PA Photos

*w*: B.OD's 'bod' as he shows off the scar from the dislocated shoulder ustained in the incident.

© Cleva

*Above*: By Royal appointment? Despite his injury Brian stayed on with the Lions squ in New Zealand to play an important off-field role (*left to right*) – Sir Clive Woodward and players Will Greenwood, Prince William, Gordon Bulloch, Gareth Thomas and B

*Below left*: Alastair Campbell, the political spin doctor turned controversial media advisor on the tour.

*Below right*: Offering consolation to Shane Byrne (*centre*) and Shane Horgan after the the third and final test, a 38-19 defeat to end a disastrous tour.                    © PA P

*ve*: Celebrating winning the Triple Crown in 2006 after a dramatic victory
: England.

*w*: Brian is ecstatic after Leinster win the last ever club game to be
ed at Lansdowne Road.

© *PA Photos*

*Above*: The cream of British and Irish sportsmen (*from left-right*) –
Brian, Phillips Idowu, Alastair Cook, Micah Richards and Marlon Devonish.

*Below*: Triple Crown victory once more in 2007 – though the Irish were to be
cruelly denied the Championship.

ve: Brian scores a try against Namibia in a shaky start to Ireland's 2007
d Cup campaign.

w: And the tournament doesn't get much better as Ireland are eliminated
rgentina. © PA Photos

GAIETY THEATRE
17TH FEBRUARY 2008

...ith his beautiful
...lfriend, actress Amy
...bberman, at the Irish
...m and Television Awards.

*A Photos*

wasn't long into the second half before Dan Carter ensured the Lions were out of the game for good. Within minutes, he had kicked a penalty, which was followed by a memorable solo try that he duly converted from the right touchline.

The Lions were deflated, although they weren't going to give up without a fight, but 10 minutes of superb pressure that followed produced nothing. The All Blacks defence was just too strong. Just before the hour mark, Jonny hobbled off after a tackle on Tana went badly wrong, causing a 'stinger' injury to his already fragile right shoulder.

They got a consolation try through Simon Easterby but in the final quarter the All Blacks turned on the class, scoring a further two tries, one coming from Dan Carter to cap off what was probably the greatest performance of his career to date, followed by a short-range effort from McCaw to seal a 48–18 victory, securing the series in the process.

It was all over. The Lions had blown it. There would be time in the weeks and months ahead for a detailed post-mortem, but, for now, everyone involved was devastated. Every single player who boarded that plane to New Zealand all those weeks before had worked hard to earn their place in the squad. The backroom staff had left nothing to chance, and it was difficult to see how they could have prepared better at this stage.

Yet, despite everything, things just hadn't clicked. There were numerous problems the Lions could look to. The line-out was generally poor, as was the scrummaging. The defence looked brilliant in patches but poor communication often let the All Blacks through at vital moments.

Even though Brian was watching from the sidelines that night, the defeat affected him more than most. During the past week, he had taken his role as non-playing captain seriously and was on hand to give the boys guidance and advice. He had lived and breathed the Lions over the past few months, and staying in the same hotel as them and being surrounded by the same old faces meant he couldn't detach himself from them easily.

As soon as the final whistle had blown, Brian headed down to the changing room to be with his team-mates. They all felt the pain as much as he did. After all, this tour was the pinnacle of their rugby-playing careers for many of them. They could not realistically hope to collect a World Cup winners' medal before they retired, so, for them, this tour was as good as things got.

Prince William had arrived in New Zealand a few days earlier and had met Brian in the hotel the day before the game. The Prince went down to the changing room to console the Lions, where Brian greeted him with: 'Howaya, Willie!' Royal protocol was clearly not at the top of his priority list at the time.

## Moving On

The Prince sat down and chatted to Brian about the game for 10 minutes, and the boys generally seemed to appreciate the gesture of his coming down and consoling them.

When they got back to the hotel, the mood seemed to ease somewhat and the atmosphere was nowhere near as grim as it had been following the previous week's defeat. Many of the players had given a decent account of themselves and they were far from disgraced in that night's game. Clive said in the post-match press conference that they had just been beaten by a stronger, better side. Brian, meanwhile, had come to the conclusion that the side had not yet peaked and that they probably should have had five weeks together before the Test series began. He told his team-mates that, if the Test series was starting again right now, it would be far closer.

The media, meanwhile, were far less forgiving, and the Sunday papers were full of condemnation of the Lions. Sir Clive, who had been hailed as a national hero less than two years before, bore the brunt of the criticism for his team selection, coaching methods and choice of captain. So many prominent journalists seemed very wise after the event.

Brian decided to hit the town that night and drown his sorrows. He and several of the Lions met up with the All Blacks and they enjoyed spending some time socialising together. The spear-tackle incident was the last thing on most of their minds, and it wasn't long before Brian realised that he actually liked a lot of the All Blacks as people. At one point in the night, he caught Justin Marshall's eye and was about to go up to him and thank him for being the man who came up to see if he was OK after that tackle. But then he decided this probably wasn't the right moment. It could reignite the situation at a time when everyone was getting along well and enjoying one another's company.

Instead, the two men talked for a while about Justin's upcoming move to Leeds. Brian soon found out that Justin was a massive golfer, so he took the opportunity to invite him to stay at his house if he fancied a short golfing break in Ireland. It seemed the most appropriate thing to do at the time, and it was his way of letting Justin know that he had a great deal of respect for him as a person.

By the beginning of the following week, Brian just wanted to go home. Looking out of his hotel window, he became depressed by the grey weather and felt it was a waste of time his being there. For the first time, he felt like a hanger-on, a spare part who served no purpose. He felt a fraud for accepting payment and believed he didn't deserve to be there. The one thing he could do to put that right was head straight for the gym and train hard to make amends as soon as possible, but he could not even consider doing this until after his operation.

He also came to realise that he felt very different on this visit to New Zealand from his previous trip there with Ireland. Put simply, he wasn't enjoying it anywhere near as much. He had become increasingly aware of a nasty edge to the public's passion for rugby. Every time he came out of a pub or café, he would be subjected to loutish and drunken abuse from supporters, something he didn't recall happening when he was last there three years earlier.

In Brian's view, the public's passion for rugby was bordering on an unhealthy obsession, to the extent that it dominates national life. He read that after the Christchurch Test there were 22 arrests, all of them New Zealanders. Some of the Lions fans got pretty drunk that night, but not one of them crossed the line and became nasty with it. Brian didn't think this was a coincidence.

He was also fed up with the attitude of virtually all of New Zealand's press, who seemed absurdly biased in their reporting of matches, to the extent that they were completely unrecognisable from the game he had just played in. All of this, he felt, was not a healthy approach to have. He was increasingly aware of the need to have a life outside rugby, and felt the New Zealand public could learn from his changing attitude. He thought that maybe things could be better if they had perhaps a few other national sports that captured the public's imagination.

These days, cricket came a very distant second to rugby in the minds of the people. There was very little else that the nation got passionate about apart from rugby, and this, he felt, meant that winning games became too important – it was no longer just a sport.

Brian's mood lifted slightly later that day when he read an article by Lions veteran JPR Williams, who said that the problem with the 2005 Lions was that they did not sleep together! This made Brian chuckle, but, reading on, he soon realised that there was a very interesting point behind it.

JPR was making the point that, in his day, sharing a room with a player from another country and travelling around on old planes and trains helped to create a really tight squad. Brian knew that there was probably a lot of truth in what he was saying. A close-knit squad who spend virtually every minute of the day together undoubtedly feel more like a team when out on the field.

But Brian also knew that this was the professional era, and there could be no going back to the old ways, and any attempts to deliberately make life difficult for the players would not be appreciated. He also remembered how relieved he felt on that first day of the tour when he found out that players would each be having their own room.

He began to feel a lot better about things the following day when he went with his mate, Prince Willie, to visit the

Starship Children's Hospital in Auckland, accompanied by Andrew Sheridan. Not for the first time on this tour, Brian experienced something that made losing a game of rugby seem not all that important after all.

The Prince took the lead and it soon became clear that he had inherited his mother's incredible gift for being able to communicate with children. Seeing these sick children being so positive as they fought serious illnesses came as a stern reminder to Brian that there were people in this world, not too far away from where the rugby was going on, who were going through a far tougher time than he was.

Brian spent the afternoon relaxing with Glenda, before making his way to the stadium for the Lions' match against Auckland, which was played in torrential rain. The home side put out virtually their entire Super 12 team, so this was always going to be a tough challenge. This Auckland team were by far the strongest midweek opposition they had experienced all tour.

The Lions took the lead through a Charlie Hodgson penalty after four minutes. It soon became clear that Auckland were up for this challenge when they bravely opted for tap-penalty moves rather than kicks for goal on three separate occasions in the first half, but the Lions defence just about did enough to hold up.

Charlie, who had been playing well enough to warrant a place in the Test side, was forced off injured midway through the first half, and was replaced by Ronan, who added another three points straight away. But Auckland quickly replied with three points of their own through Brent Ward.

Martyn Williams was denied what looked like a certain try when he was taken out off the ball right under the posts. Shortly before half-time, the Lions finally scored following an impressive jinking run from Mark Cueto, before crossing to Martyn to finish off a perfectly executed manoeuvre, making the score 14–3 at the break.

A penalty against Gordon D'Arcy allowed Brent Ward to kick Auckland back into the game early in the second half, which seemed to give the home side momentum as they controlled possession for most of the remainder of the match. Some clever passing by Auckland created gaps in the Lions line, and their persistence paid off when Isa Nacewa crossed for a try, which was duly converted.

The Lions were now well and truly on the back foot and had to defend manically to avoid throwing the game away. They soon conceded another penalty with just 11 minutes to go, but Ward's kick hit the post. This was proving to be a real nail-biter.

Ronan kicked a penalty with just five minutes to go which put some space between the sides, but there really was no telling which team were the club side in the second half. They were evenly matched throughout; indeed, if anything, it could easily be argued that Auckland were the stronger of the teams. Nevertheless, the midweek Lions were delighted to have won a tough battle in awkward, slippery conditions. Brian was especially happy with the result, as from where he was sitting he could see thousands of loyal Lions fans who had braved the conditions and had been soaked right through. If anyone deserved to see the team win, it was them.

Following the game, Brian joined the team in the 'Midweek Massive' party, which they had been planning for some time. It was a heavy night on the town that was well deserved. Even Prince William received an invite, though he couldn't attend due to other engagements. The Southland game aside, the midweek boys had done themselves proud throughout the tour, and coach Ian McGeechan aided by Gareth Jenkins could be very proud of what they had achieved with the players.

The following day, Brian couldn't help but think that separating the Test and midweek teams during training sessions had been a major mistake. It is true that there had been a very chaotic squad session in the first week, and that Clive had decided to split them up from then on, but by now Brian had reached the conclusion that they could learn a lot from each other and that it would have helped develop a feeling of being a complete squad.

On the evening of 7 July, Brian received yet another

poignant reminder that there was more to life than rugby when he turned on the television in his room to discover that suicide bombers had struck London. He headed downstairs and met up with the rest of the squad, many of whom were frantically phoning home to make sure none of their loved ones was missing. Fortunately for them, everyone they knew was safe but as the death toll rose by the hour the whole squad got a sharp reminder that the upcoming Test was only a game.

With the relief of knowing that none of the boys had been directly affected by the terrible news, Brian proceeded with his evening's plans and enjoyed a night's social eating and drinking with some friends who had come over from Ireland, who had probably booked their tickets expecting to see him captaining the Lions in what may well have been a series-deciding Test match. Still, it wasn't to be and Brian decided to just enjoy their company for the evening and have a few drinks instead.

The following night, which was the night before the game, Brian decided that he would be doing more harm than good if he were to stay around the Test squad. He had been invited for a few 'quiet drinks' with Jason Leonard. He knew full well what this meant. Jason simply didn't do 'quiet drinks' and this would inevitably lead to a good drinking session. Brian couldn't think of a single good reason not to accept the offer, and so the two headed off.

## Moving On

Once again, Brian took his seat in the stand in Auckland for the final Test. Yes, the series was lost, but there was still a lot to play for in this game. Every single member of the squad wanted to avoid being forever labelled as part of the Lions squad that lost every Test match on tour. They were playing for pride, and for their reputations as world-class rugby players.

Before kick-off, there was an impeccably observed minute's silence in memory of those who had lost their lives in the London bombings. When the referee blew his whistle to start the game, it was the Lions who took the initiative, when Stephen Jones kicked a penalty after just three minutes.

They should have scored their first try early on, after a searing Josh Lewsey break down the left touchline, and a powerful run from Gethin Jenkins set up a promising position, but Irish lock Donncha O'Callaghan spurned a clear four-man overlap to his right.

Stephen Jones added another three points after their old friend Tana was sin-binned for lying on the ball, deliberately slowing down possession. If the Lions thought that the All Blacks had gone to sleep, they were about to be given a blunt reminder that they were playing the best Test side in the world.

A surge from number eight Sione Lauaki fed Conrad Smith, who beat Geordan Murphy and Mark Cueto to romp home under the posts. With Dan Carter injured, it was left to the debutant Luke McAlister to take the kick. He duly added two points with the easy conversion.

It wasn't long until the All Blacks added a second, when Dwayne Peel fumbled McAllister's grubber kick, allowing Williams in for a try. The Lions fought back almost immediately when Stephen Jones added another penalty on 23 minutes.

The opening quarter had been played in cold, but dry weather, but all that was about to change. Without warning, the heavens opened and torrential rain poured down on Eden Park, turning the pitch into a waterlogged mud bath in no time at all. Both sides, but especially the Lions, struggled to adapt to the severity of the conditions as passes were fumbled due to the greasy ball.

A relatively straightforward Jones penalty hit the post and stayed out, and things went from bad to worse a few minutes later when a Josh Lewsey error resulted in a try for Tana right under the posts.

A passionate half-time team talk from Clive didn't have the desired effect, and their spirits were deflated still further early in the second half when Tana scored his second try of the game. Could things get any worse? The hosts soon added a fifth try, but mercifully for the Lions this was disallowed after Jerry Collins was sin-binned for an off-the-ball tackle on Jones.

This gave the Lions some inspiration, and a prolonged spell camped on New Zealand's line was eventually rewarded with a try for Lewis Moody. This was to prove nothing more than a consolation try, however, as from then on the Lions seemed tired, sluggish and eager to get on the plane home. This was capped off when Rico Gear chased a kick at the death to score one more try, bringing the final score to 38–19.

Unfortunately, any bitterness between the two camps was not eased following the final whistle. Clive and Graham Henry had been at loggerheads since Henry was put in charge of the Lions tour four years previously. Clive had been highly critical of many aspects of Henry's preparation for that tour. In his post-match interview, Henry was clearly in no mood to extend an olive branch. He said, '2001 was a blessing for me because I wouldn't be sitting here now if it wasn't for 2001, so I should thank the people for the ribbing because it pushed me back to New Zealand quicker than I probably would have come back.'

Clive, maintaining a degree of dignity, urged caution on the part of the New Zealand rugby-loving public. He warned them not to get too carried away with this tour win, and that they could not take winning the World Cup in two years' time for granted. Clive said, 'I would offer a caution on the New Zealand team. When I see them going through the quarter-finals and semi-finals and win a World Cup, then it is time to celebrate, because it is a very tough tournament. The only time you

can judge teams like New Zealand is when you arrive at
World Cups when everyone has had the same degree of
preparation.' Clive's words would turn out to be a sound
prophecy, but they sounded like sour grapes to the New
Zealanders at the time.

Brian joined the rest of the squad in attending the
after-match function, but he wasn't really in the mood
for polite company and left as soon as it was respectful
to do so. Some of the guys, such as Gareth Thomas, had
been suffering with a touch of flu and Brian felt that he
might have been coming down with it.

He headed back to the hotel and turned in for the
night, knowing that he had a very long day's flying home
ahead of him. When he got up the following morning,
some of the boys were still heading in after a wild night
out with the New Zealand players. He didn't especially
mind them going out and enjoying themselves; after all,
the series had really been lost the week before. But, for
him, there was no hiding the disappointment he felt, not
just for himself but for the whole camp. A career-
defining tour, one that, on paper, provided the Lions
with their best hope of winning a series in New Zealand
in decades, had come to nothing.

Brian had started the tour intending to mix with the
All Blacks far more than had been possible, through a
combination of the bad blood that had emerged between
them and the constraints of time. This was just another

of the disappointments he had to come to terms with. All those months earlier when Brian and Clive talked at his home in Henley, the two men agreed that they should make every effort to enjoy the experience of being in New Zealand and to soak up the culture and attractions the country had to offer.

The reality was far different. Brian had not enjoyed being there at all for much of the time. The only part of New Zealand he really liked was Wellington, which he considered a place he could emigrate to one day. He wished there had been far more opportunities to explore New Zealand's rich and ancient culture, but the sheer intensity of the tour, and his determination to remain completely focused on the rugby in the lead-up to the big games, made that impossible. There were no sightseeing trips.

He had felt humbled when visiting sick children with Prince William, and had enjoyed the precious few chances to watch the schoolchildren train, but there had been few other excursions. The way Brian was feeling now, he just wanted to get on the plane and begin the long journey home. Luckily, having an early night meant that he was in far better shape for a long flight than most of the squad were, which would involve stop-offs in Sydney, Singapore and Heathrow, before finally touching down in Dublin. Brian couldn't wait to get back home.

It was a warm summer's day in Dublin and Brian was back where he wanted to be. He organised a barbecue to celebrate his homecoming, which was attended by a select group of friends. He was feeling mighty relieved to be back home, and glad that at long last the tour was behind him. His shoulder was feeling surprisingly good, perhaps a little too good really. As he enjoyed the evening, he completely forgot about his shoulder, until he dropped a bread roll and moved suddenly to catch it, and got a painful reminder that he was suffering from a serious injury.

The following day, he did the sensible thing and saw a local specialist. The diagnosis was exactly the same as in New Zealand. Eager to get it over with and move on, Brian booked himself in for the op that coming Friday.

In the few days he had before he was to go into hospital, Brian began making preparations for his house move. He had decided to have a new house built, and, upon visiting the site, he was surprised to see the plot cleared and the foundations already laid. The plan was to move in by Christmas. He got talking to one of the builders who said that his local had put up a poster with a picture of Tana that read underneath: 'Barred for life from these premises.' Another of the workers, a real giant of a man, told Brian that he should sue for GBH, and he wasn't joking.

As Brian was about to find out, this man's strong feelings on the incident were by no means rare. With some time on his hands, Brian started reading up on the British and Irish newspapers' take on the saga. He had heard that the story had been huge back home, but it was hard for him not to become blinkered by the very biased, one-eyed perspective given by the New Zealand press. When he analysed what had been written in his absence, even he was shocked by the strength of feeling about it. That said, he was unhappy with the way in which so many articles had been mixed up with Alastair Campbell's supposed spinning of the story. In Brian's mind, nothing could have been further from the truth, as Alastair had nothing whatsoever to do with the publicity that followed. It was Brian who decided to release a press statement on the night of the incident and it was he who showed up at the press conference the following morning and spoke from the heart. It also seemed absurd to link Alastair to any of the sentiments that came from the subsequent New Zealand press conferences where Graham Henry and his chums did everything they could to play down the incident.

Brian checked into the hospital the night before the operation. The hospital staff talked him through the procedure, and he found out that the operation was nicknamed the 'shark's bite' because it leaves a deep, prominent scar. The plan was to open up the shoulder and reset the joint before tightening it up with 16 staples, allowing the ligaments to grow in exactly the right position so that the shoulder regains full strength. The operation was deemed a success but it was clear that Brian would probably miss the autumn internationals, and making it on to the field for Leinster at Christmas was a far more realistic target.

He was home in two days and made the decision to hide from the public view until he was fully recovered. Over the next few months, he would be looking to spend more time with Glenda – she certainly deserved to be spoiled a bit by him after the few months she'd endured with him. He would also be taking a far keener interest than he otherwise would in the construction of his new home, visiting on an almost daily basis to see how it was coming along. The next few months were about sitting back and doing very little, giving the shoulder every chance to get back to full strength.

The year had promised so much for Brian, and looked set to be the most successful of his career, yet it had delivered absolutely nothing. Leinster had blown their chance of European glory, and the Ireland team had seen their prospects of winning the Grand Slam fall apart. The Lions tour, which had been planned to perfection in Brian's eyes, cruelly fell apart for him within a matter of seconds of the first Test kicking off. But there was little he could do about it now. All he could do was put his feet up, allow his body time to heal and plot his comeback at the end of the year.

# CHAPTER 8

# BACK IN
# BUSINESS

**B**rian's aim of maintaining a low profile during his recuperation didn't exactly go according to plan. In a number of interviews, he had hinted that at some point in his career he would like to play his club rugby in France. This was not intended as some kind of clue that he was in advanced negotiations with a French club, but the media, especially in Ireland, began speculating that he would be leaving Leinster when his contract expired in the summer.

In truth, Brian's reasons for wanting to move to France at some point were simple. The attacking, physical style of rugby the French clubs tend to play particularly suits his game, and he was growing a bit tired of the weather back home. Then again, he was having a brand-new home built to his specifications, so that might have been taken as a hint that he wasn't planning to move away any time soon. The speculation gathered pace in September when Brian was spotted in the crowd for a game between Biarritz and Stade Francais. There were persistent rumours that he was there to discuss a contract with Biarritz, though it is equally plausible that he was there to enjoy the rugby and kill some time as he recovered from injury.

The IRFU repeatedly stated that they wanted to keep as many of their players as possible playing in Ireland. Yes, it is true that there were several players plying their trade for English clubs and Simon Easterby was playing for Llanelli, but, as captain and their most prominent star, Brian was the jewel in their crown and it was deemed important for the good of the national game that he remained within their domestic setup.

For the next few months, Brian's club future remained in a state of limbo as he neither signed a new contract with Leinster nor committed himself to a French club. However, new Leinster coach Michael Cheika appointed Brian club captain, taking over from Reggie Corrigan for the upcoming season. He had made it clear to his new coach that he intended to be fully involved with the team despite his other commitments, and Michael couldn't hide his delight at the unveiling press conference that a man who was held in such high esteem as Brian was had accepted this honour. Brian didn't take on this commitment lightly, and from this point onwards he wanted to remain at Leinster for the foreseeable future, provided the right contract could be agreed.

Although he was obviously in no fit state to take part in day-to-day training, he was impressed with the changes Michael had brought in during his short time there and felt that after years of stalemate both he and the club were going places, and would be serious competitors for major silverware in the upcoming season.

In November, he had to settle for a seat in the stand at Lansdowne Road as Ireland took on New Zealand in the first of the autumn internationals. The Ireland squad, along with the pundits, believed they stood a chance of giving the All Blacks a run for their money to go some way towards getting revenge for the Lions tour flop. The visitors clearly didn't share the sense of occasion as coach Graham Henry fielded a completely different side to the one that had just defeated Wales, with a few less familiar names in the squad. That's not to say there weren't plenty of world-class players taking to the field to perform the haka in front of 42,000 mostly Irish fans that day.

Ireland made a strong start but soon struggled to get out of their own half, and it quickly became clear that the side was missing Brian and there was a considerable gulf in class between the sides. After just 10 minutes, the All Blacks forced a scrum deep inside Ireland's 22, which resulted in a soft try for Sivivatu. They added a second 12 minutes later when some superb long passing allowed scrum-half Piri Weepu to score. The conversion was missed, but Ireland were up against it and conceded a penalty right under the posts a few minutes later, which was easily kicked over the bar by Nick Evans. Ireland produced a rare attack of their own five minutes later thanks to a Gordon D'Arcy burst but Geordan Murphy spilled the centre's less than accurate pass. The visitors were soon awarded another penalty deep inside the Irish half, which added another three points to their tally, sealing their authority on the game. The Irish defence was poor, and Sivivatu had acres of space when he scored his second just before half-time, making the score at the break 25–0.

Eddie O'Sullivan's team talk didn't have the desired effect as the second half brought more of the same. New Zealand scored two quick penalties to rub salt in the wound, but something was about to happen that would have supporters having flashbacks to the tackle that ended Brian's Lions tour a few months ago. Ma'a Nonu performed an extremely violent tackle on Gordon D'Arcy which greatly upset the crowd, though match referee Jonathan Kaplan decided that it did not even warrant a yellow card. The incident gave Ireland a new lease of life as they sought to punish the All Blacks for the tackle, but their best opportunity to score was lost when Ronan failed to utilise a five-on-three overlap. After that, New Zealand reasserted their control of the game. The video referee was called to pass judgement on two close calls for Doug Howlett and Nonu, deciding both were not tries. Eventually, they did manage to score again through Howlett, putting the game well beyond Ireland's reach. The hosts did eventually get a consolation try through Horan that was duly converted, saving the hosts from the humiliation of failing to register a score. However, there was no denying the team's disappointment in being unable to exact any kind of meaningful revenge on the All Blacks, and seeing some of the less pleasant aspects of the Kiwi game being played out on Irish soil left a bitter taste in the mouth and did little to lift Brian's spirits.

The truth was that, without Brian, Ireland were no match for New Zealand's sheer physical presence. There was no hiding the fact that Ireland had suffered a heavy defeat by what was essentially New Zealand's second-string side. This concerned both Eddie and Brian significantly. How could a side that, at the start of the year was being touted as potential Grand Slam winners and among the world's best sides, have fallen so far backwards in such a short space of time? It could not all be put down to Brian being out injured. There were clearly a number of areas that needed reviewing.

A week later, there was a chance to put things right when they took on an out-of-sorts Australia side. Eddie decided to stick with much the same side that crashed the week before; however, he did allow the young Ulster centre Andrew Trimble the chance to make his Test debut. Once again, Eddie decided to keep faith with Simon Easterby in Brian's absence. Ireland looked the better side during the opening exchanges, although neither team produced anything approaching earth-shattering rugby. Ireland took the lead after seven minutes when Ronan kicked over a penalty. A superb Johnny O'Connor run exposed the fragile nature of the Australian defence but his pass could not find Gordon D'Arcy, blowing a golden opportunity to score the first try of the game. A heavy double-hit saw Malcolm O'Kelly knocked out for the count, but Ronan failed to make the most of the penalty that followed. His opposite number Mat Rogers gleefully accepted a quick chance to reply on 26 minutes when Ireland strayed offside, and he levelled the scores at three a piece. Shortly before half-time, Ronan made up for his earlier mistake by putting a penalty over to put the hosts 6–3 up at half-time.

It wasn't pretty, but at last Ireland were looking like a team that could beat one of the big names in world rugby. Brian would not have been satisfied with what he saw of the first half. Yes, they were winning, but the lead could – and should – have been much more convincing. Tommy

Bowe missed out on a glorious chance for the first try through no fault of his own in the closing stages of the first half. A sweeping move off a set scrum in the right corner saw Ronan, Gordon and Geordan Murphy combine to arch Ireland out to the left flank and into space – a killer pass was called for but, with Bowe haring up the touchline, Murphy's offload was far too high and found touch.

Straight after the break, Rogers levelled the scores once more with a simple penalty. Just five minutes later, Ireland failed to take Drew Mitchell out of the game, and as he stayed on his feet the support players pushed him over the line for a try. From then on, the game started to slip away from Ireland. David Humphreys came on for Ronan and soon converted a penalty, but that was to signal Australia's revival. Ireland's line-out was shambolic, allowing Chris Latham to charge through a gap and score from 50 metres out. Things went from bad to worse when Humphreys saw his pass intercepted by Mitchell who ran down the field, and, although he was initially stopped by Bowe, he found his feet once more to score his second of the game. Once again, Ireland had to settle for a consolation score that finally came four minutes from the end after a promising move saw Shane Horgan touch down. However, Australia were to have the final say when Rogers converted his third penalty to make the final score 30–14, ending Australia's seven-game losing streak.

It would have been hard for Brian to put his finger on exactly what went wrong in that game. Australia looked very beatable and there were some superb individual performances from Irish players. But, as a team, they did not gel and this was to be their downfall. Key areas such as the scrum and the line-out clearly required a great deal of work before the upcoming Six Nations campaign. There was one more autumn international to come, against Romania the following week, and, despite the weak opposition, Eddie decided to stick with the same players who had failed to gel in the previous two games. This call led to his receiving a great deal of stick in the Irish media in the days leading up to the game, with numerous journalists calling for him to drop John Hayes and Shane Byrne, who many believed had been poor scrummagers for some time. However, one notable change saw David Humphreys attempt to fill Brian's boots as captain.

At a blustery Lansdowne Road, Ireland started the game poorly, failing to assert their superiority over the amateur opposition. Despite the captain successfully kicking a penalty early on, two conceded penalties of their own saw Romania leading 6–3 after 12 minutes. Superb individual performances were the order of the day when a well-timed break by Geordan Murphy, followed by a perfect pass to Trimble, allowed the youngster to score on 22 minutes, which Humphreys then converted. Neil Best, Ireland's most consistent player in the opening half, then rounded off a period of pressure three minutes before the interval when he broke through a couple of weak tackles to notch the home side's second try. The subsequent conversion gave Ireland a 17–6 lead at half-time.

Ireland made a sloppy start to the second half and it was only a quick-thinking intervention from Geordan that stopped the visitors scoring a try of their own after Humphreys's attempted clearance had been charged down. Trimble soon notched up his second try of the game, earning him the man of the match award for his superb display in only his second Test. Two Romanian penalties in quick succession reduced the deficit to 24–12, and for a short while it looked as though one moment of good fortune for the visitors could make the scoreline uncomfortably close.

However, as the match wore on, fitness levels began to tell and Johnny O'Connor pushed through some sloppy tackling to score for Ireland. The conversion made the score 32–12 and finally there was some daylight between the two sides. The remainder of the match didn't resemble an international game of rugby as both sides were guilty of some very poor tackling. Ireland were on the defensive for sustained periods and the Romanians came uncomfortably close to scoring on more than one occasion. Poor tackling by the visitors allowed late tries from Geordan and Girvan Dempsey but in all honesty the 43–12 final score flattered Ireland, and fans would have expected a far wider gulf between such mismatched sides.

It was now time to go back to club duty until the following year's Six Nations but Brian knew that there would have to be some very hard work put in if Ireland were to be serious contenders for the upcoming Six Nations. The Romania game had reinforced the fact that there were some brilliant individual performers wearing the green jersey, but they did not gel as a team. If they could tighten up their line-out, improve their scrummaging, pass precisely and get the tackling right, they would be one of the world's very best teams. This was clearly frustrating for Brian to watch, but only made him more determined to put things right once his shoulder was sorted out.

In early December 2005 came the news that, after months of speculation, Brian had signed a new contract with Leinster that would keep him at the club until after the 2007 World Cup. This was far from the ideal solution the IRFU had wanted, as they sought to keep him committed to playing in Ireland for a far longer period. But for Brian this was an ideal compromise. It would keep him at the province for the foreseeable future, ending the unhelpful speculation, and allow him time to settle into his new home. On the other hand, the length of this contract would allow him to fulfil his dream to play for a French club while still at his peak in less than two years' time.

Meanwhile, his recovery was going to plan and he was on course to be playing again soon. On Boxing Day, rugby fans from all over Ireland got the Christmas present they really wanted when Brian was named on the bench for Leinster's Celtic League fixture at Ulster. He came on to applause from the whole crowd after 50 minutes. He didn't get too involved in the half-hour he played, but his presence spurred on Gordon and Girvan to score a try each to turn a half-time deficit into a 24–19 victory for Leinster away from home. Brian knew that it would take five or six games for him to be completely match-fit and that he could not take anything for granted at this stage. But after months of misery and some unhelpful speculation about his future, it just felt good to be playing rugby once again.

On New Year's Eve came the traditional battle against arch rivals Munster, now coached by Declan Kidney. Brian's first start at home was greeted by a Celtic League record crowd of 14,155. These matches were always fiercely fought affairs and this was to prove no different. Leinster scored the first try when young hooker Brian Blaney got over from a line-out drive. A Felipe Contepomi penalty was soon added, but Munster were allowed back into the game when Ronan scored two penalties in quick succession. Shane Horgan scored for Leinster shortly before the break after a superb run that saw him resist tackles from Anthony Horgan and David Wallace to put the ball down in the right corner. Contepomi added the two points with a superb kick taken at an awkward angle, and added his third penalty of the game in first-half stoppage time.

In the second half, Munster stepped up the pace and reminded Leinster that these games aren't over until they're over, and on 65 minutes O'Connell spurned tackles from Easterby and Blaney, and the resulting conversion cut Leinster's lead to just six points. Contepomi was the star of the game and on 74 minutes he chipped the ball over Anthony Foley and beat the cover right beneath the posts, which he duly converted. Munster pulled one back through Trevor Halstead to make for a tense final few minutes, but Contepomi raced on to a loose ball 35 metres out and beat the covering Horgan and Halstead to score at the corner flag, making the final score 35–23.

This was a quiet game by Brian's standards. He didn't want to take any chances and so didn't become too involved. He was far from fully fit and it was left to others to take the star roles, but this famous victory over their old rivals made it a happy ending to what had been a pretty miserable year.

The New Year arrived, and inevitably attention soon

turned to the 2006 Six Nations. As usual, the squad met up at the City West hotel in Dublin several weeks in advance to prepare for the long campaign that lay ahead. Brian was getting fitter by the day, and was on course to be back to full fitness when the time came to lead his men out to battle against Italy at Lansdowne Road in just a few weeks' time.

Eddie knew he had his work cut out in the weeks ahead, but it was a massive consolation to him to have a squad of players, who, as individuals, were truly among the world's best. His task was to coach them to think and play like a team, which had been their downfall in the autumn internationals. Training was well structured and intense during those few weeks. The line-out was regarded as an area where games were won and lost and in the Tests against New Zealand and Australia this was exposed as a major frailty in Ireland's armoury. The only way this was ever going to be put right was through practising the drills and learning the line-out calls by heart.

The first match was at home against Italy, but Brian and Eddie both knew only too well that the days of Italy being the whipping boys of the tournament were past and they could not afford a repeat of the previous year's sluggish performance if they were to secure victory. Brian led the team out at Lansdowne Road feeling confident that they had prepared well and this would be the year that the squad's potential would be revealed and

Ireland would take the Six Nations by storm. Yes, he had felt exactly the same way the previous year, but this time he, and a few of the others, had matured considerably as players and this would show through on the pitch.

However, things didn't exactly go according to plan. A fired-up Italian side pegged Ireland back and didn't allow them to play the wide, expansive game they were looking to play. It became clear very early on that there were still serious problems with the line-out and it was going to be a tough 80 minutes.

Italy took the lead early on when the excellent Ramiro Pez tapped over a penalty. The first Ireland try came when O'Connell managed to steal the ball from the Italian line-out, before passing to the debutant Jerry Flannery, who was hauled over the line. Ronan added the conversion to put a bit of breathing space between the sides, which went some way towards making up for the 40-metre penalty he had fluffed a few minutes earlier.

The game was evenly poised and the visitors regained the lead on 29 minutes when Pez found a gap between Ronan and Gordon to set up a try for Mauro Bergamasco. Pez, who was having the game of his life, added the two points. However, he let his enthusiasm get the better of him just a few minutes later when he was yellow-carded for a late tackle, allowing Ronan to add three points from the penalty that followed to bring the scores level at half-time at 10 points a piece.

Paul Griffen edged the Azzuri ahead on the restart. It was a statement of intent, as they stretched the Irish defence in the period of play that followed. Eventually, Ireland managed to find a little more space in an often cluttered midfield and Gordon started causing problems for the Italian defence. But it was Bowe who eventually scored when he received an excellent cross-field kick from Ronan before outwitting the defence to score. Ronan converted and knocked over a couple of penalties with Pez also squeezing in one of his own as Ireland moved seven points ahead. However, the previously excellent Pez was struggling to keep his concentration and missed a simple penalty that would have made the final minutes very tense. Ronan soon made the game safe for Ireland with his fourth penalty in the 76th minute.

It was a victory, and a win is always a win, but Brian knew that this had been a quiet game by his standards and there was still a great deal of work to be done if they were to defeat the stronger sides – and, with a trip to the Stade de France just a week away, there was work to be done. If Italy's backs had been stronger, it would have been a very different story. Brian's preparation hadn't been ideal and, while he was now back in the peak of physical fitness, he lacked match practice and this showed on the field. The squad watched the video of the game with Eddie during the week and looked at the areas that needed tightening up ahead of the upcoming games. It was the same old story – untidy line-out, gaps in the defence and loss of concentration at key times.

That said, Brian was looking forward to the match against France. Their style of rugby suited his game and a strong, physical encounter was probably exactly what was needed in order for him to reach full match fitness. Brian led the team on to the field feeling geared up for the challenge. Matches away at France in front of a full house are always special occasions and Brian had been gearing himself up for this fixture all week. However, it wasn't long before things started to go wrong once more. Bowe's slip in midfield after just three minutes handed possession to the French and Aurelien Rougerie touched down in the corner after beating Geordan. Ireland didn't lie down and die and were awarded a penalty of their own, but disaster soon struck. The decision to take the tap penalty instead of kicking an easy three points rebounded disastrously when Denis Leamy and Geordan got in each other's way, allowing Frederic Michalak to grab the ball and begin a charge down the other end of the field before supplying Olivier Magne with the scoring pass.

This had been a disastrous tactical decision and meant the game was all but lost after just 15 minutes. Ronan was having a howler of a game. After missing a penalty, his clearance kick on 18 minutes was charged down by David Marty who went on to score another French try.

Ireland's fighting spirit was needed if they were to get anything at all from this game and they responded convincingly just a minute later when Gordon crossed the French line, but it was correctly ruled out for a knock-on. Ronan and Jean-Baptiste Elissalde kicked penalties at either end before Ireland's first-half horror show was completed in the 35th minute when Murphy's speculative looping pass was intercepted by Cedric Heymans who ran in unopposed to score France's fourth try.

At half-time, the score was an embarrassing 29–3. All their hard work during the week had come to nothing. The same mistakes that had haunted the boys since the autumn internationals kept creeping back. Essentially, France were so far in front due to silly errors on the part of a handful of Irish players rather than some kind of huge gulf in ability between the sides.

If Irish fans had thought things could not get any worse, they soon did as France notched up two more tries through Heymans and Marty, with yet another awful kick from Ronan giving France their sixth try. The introduction of several replacements resulted in France picking up the loss-of-cohesion bug that Ireland had been suffering from throughout the game, and after three minutes of sustained pressure Gordon ran in an Irish try with Ronan slotting the conversion. Ireland's revival continued when replacement Donncha O'Callaghan notched another try in the 66th minute and the French lead was cut to 43–31. Andrew Trimble touched down with 11 minutes remaining, with Ronan adding both conversions, going at least some way towards making up for his appalling first-half performance. It was going to be a tense end to a game that was suddenly looking winnable for Brian's men. However, the French regained their composure and held on for a win.

Once again, Brian had not been the centre of attention during the game but he took great heart from his side's display in the final half-hour. The defeat definitely hurt, but the truth was that Ireland had dominated the final part of the game and Brian knew that, if they could maintain those levels of commitment and discipline for the three games that remained, they would still be in with a shout of winning the Championship. Within a day, Brian had moved on from the defeat and began preparing for the home fixture against Wales. He remembered that incredible day in Cardiff during the final weekend of the previous year's Championship and was keen to exact revenge. He was also aware that the Welsh camp had been in disarray and that this was far from being the same Wales side that had won the Grand Slam a year earlier.

Brian's old friend Mike Ruddock had resigned as Wales's coach just days after their unconvincing win at home to Scotland. Mike had cited family reasons for his resignation but there had been ongoing rumours of a rift with Gareth Thomas, who made little secret of the fact that he had been having serious clashes with his coach.

This was a difficult issue for Brian to deal with. He had a huge amount of affection for Mike from his days as a young player, yet he had also become close to Gareth during the previous summer's Lions tour and had been impressed with his captaincy when called upon, which made it very hard for him to make any kind of judgement on the issue. What was clear was that this was not the same Wales of a year before and this would prove a great opportunity for Brian and his men to shine among the disarray.

Wales were hit by a further massive blow when it was revealed that Gareth Thomas had been rushed to hospital and had suffered a mild stroke, ruling him out of rugby for the foreseeable future. The stress of the situation had clearly caught up with Gareth and just hours before he was taken to hospital he had been involved in a highly charged debate on Welsh television. Ireland took to the field at Lansdowne Road a more confident side than they had been at any time since the previous year's Six Nations.

However, any thoughts that the Welsh would be allowing their off-the-field problems to distract them from the task in hand were soon dispelled when Mark Jones scored after just seven minutes. Ronan pegged three points back 10 minutes later, but it was a shaky start by the home side. After 20 minutes, Brian's men started to gain control of the match and the lack of preparation by Wales was beginning to show when David Wallace scored a try from a five-metre scrum. Ronan missed an easy conversion but a penalty a few minutes later left Ireland leading 11–5 at the break.

Early in the second half, Brian made his first major contribution of the tournament when three minutes after the restart he found man of the match Shane Horgan, who then cut inside two defenders to score a superb try. Ronan didn't miss this time, and soon added another penalty to extend the Irish lead. Right at the end, scrum-half Stringer forced his way over for a try which Ronan converted, to give Ireland a sound 31–5 victory.

At last, Ireland were playing the sort of rugby Brian knew they had in them, and after the game he was typically understated as he told journalists that the convincing win had not come as a surprise to him. In his view, when the pressure came on, they produced the goods and they could take great satisfaction from that. Brian soon reminded the boys that the Championship was still very much on and, although their performance was by no means perfect, they could take a lot of pride in their overall performance.

Next up was a tricky fixture against Scotland at home. The Scots had been enjoying something of a resurgence after a lean few years, and had fired a warning shot in Brian's direction by defeating World Champions England that weekend. Their defence had been rock solid and some accurate kicking from Chris Paterson had seen them win the game 18–12. In the two-week break, Eddie's task was simply to tighten up any remaining shortcomings in their game, and prepare them in whatever way he could to play to their maximum potential for the full 80 minutes. The match against Scotland wasn't just any old game of rugby. It would be the last time Ireland took to the field in a Six Nations game at Lansdowne Road before it closed for redevelopment. This gave the game an extra edge and made Brian even more focused in the days leading up to the game.

Brian led his team out in front of an emotionally charged crowd, who wanted to give the old place a good send-off. Ireland dominated possession and territory in the first half but could not break Scotland's superb defence, who maintained the same levels of focus and accuracy that had led them to victory against England. The conditions weren't ideal following a torrential downpour just minutes before kick-off, but this only seemed to strengthen Ireland's resolve not to allow any silly mistakes to creep in on this special occasion. Ronan kicked his side in front thanks to a penalty in the second minute. He added a second three points just five minutes later but Scotland were awarded an easy kick from the resultant kick-off when Malcolm O'Kelly impeded Jason White and Paterson opened his account. Another Irish infringement allowed Paterson to draw the scores level soon after.

In tricky conditions, both sides chose to kick most of their possession and, considering the strength of both defences, there never looked like being any tries. It was going to be left to Ronan's kicking to win this awkward game. He pushed one effort wide but he soon made amends by putting one straight between the posts just minutes later, only for Paterson to draw level once more shortly afterwards. Both sides enjoyed periods of good possession in the first half but yet more heavy rain made attacking and passing play difficult, and it was another penalty from Ronan that saw Ireland lead 12–9 at half-time.

They had a good opportunity to score early in the second half when Geordan's low pass to Andrew Trimble allowed Hugo Southwell the split-second he needed to bundle the wing into touch. Another opportunity presented itself just moments later, only for Sean Lamont to pluck Paul O'Connell's pass out of the sky a metre from the line. Ireland began to dominate possession, but the Scottish defence remained rock solid and the hosts had to make do with another superbly executed penalty from Ronan to extend the lead. With seven minutes left, the visitors made what was almost their first foray of the half into Ireland's 22 but, whereas their line-out was precarious, Ireland's remained solid. This came as a mighty relief to Eddie and Brian, and at long last this aspect of the game that had gone a long way towards costing them victories over the past year finally seemed to have sorted itself out. Ronan missed one final kick, but it didn't matter and the last Championship game at the old ground ended in a 15–9 victory.

Ronan's was the only name on the scoresheet, but everyone had played their part in this victory and Brian's tactical decisions as captain had been spot on. After months in the doldrums, Ireland were on a roll. The Triple Crown was still on, and in theory they were still in with a shout of winning the Championship, although they would have to rely upon France losing against Wales for that to happen, as the points difference between them was almost certainly too great otherwise. With one game against the World Champions to go, there was a lot still to play for.

England were coming into the game following a humiliating 31–6 defeat to France in Paris. Brian knew only too well that there would not be a repeat performance at Twickenham. Yes, England were very much in a lull between World Cups but they were at their most dangerous when wounded and Brian was expecting his type of game – tough and physical – and he knew that, once again, they would face a defence that was difficult to break down. England coach Andy Robinson knew his job was on the line and that a repeat of Paris would almost certainly cost him his job.

It was England who came out of the blocks quickest when they won a penalty from a first-minute scrum that Martin Corry took quickly, and from a smartly recycled ball Jamie Noon raced on to Andy Goode's precise pass to score in the left corner. Ireland were soon let back into the game when Ben Cohen slipped when trying to deal with Brian's kick ahead, allowing Horgan to nip in and bring the scores level after just seven minutes. This game was quickly turning out to be the tight battle everyone was hoping for. A penalty kick from Ronan gave Ireland the lead five minutes later and England missed two opportunities of their own to bring the scores level. Brian should have set up a superb try for Gordon, but his pass was too high and it was an opportunity wasted. A penalty each made the score 11–8, but another incursion into the line from the impressive Geordan should have yielded more points for Ireland, but nevertheless they still went into half-time with a slender lead.

Early in the second half, Lewis Moody conceded a penalty that allowed Ronan to extend the lead to six points, but Goode kicked one over of his own almost immediately, beginning England's best passage of play.

They launched themselves at the Irish line for five minutes but appeared to have wasted their efforts when they kicked a penalty to touch and Paul O'Connell stole the line-out. But they finally found a way through when Goode's pass sent Steve Borthwick over on a great angle for his first Test try.

The game turned once more after 57 minutes when England's line-out plan fell to pieces on their own line. The throw was intended to reach the isolated Moody but Leamy intercepted to touch down, with Ronan adding the extra two points. However, two penalties in seven minutes seemed to give England the game, barring any last-minute miracles.

Cometh the hour, cometh the man, and at the very last opportunity Shane Horgan resisted Moody's attempted tackle to score right in the corner. Ireland had snatched victory from the jaws of defeat in the most breathtaking style. In the post-match interview, Brian paid tribute to his side's phenomenal spirit, saying that this was the 80 minutes of rugby he had been waiting for his team to produce. He made it clear straight away that he saw this as a stepping stone to bigger and better things and he was not prepared to rest on his laurels just yet. Yes, there would be wild celebrations that night, but already he had one eye on the World Cup that was now just 18 months away. His belief in his team's ability had proven true, and at long last the individual talents of the 15 men who wore the green jersey had gelled to create a truly world-class team.

Brian was presented with the Triple Crown trophy immediately after the game and there was no hiding the delight on his face at what had been achieved, remarkable considering the clumsy performances they had put in during the autumn internationals and in the games against Italy and France.

Upon arriving back in Ireland, Brian ended the Six Nations campaign with the traditional end-of-tournament debrief at Kehoe's bar in Dublin, which, in practice, meant a good night's drinking with the rest of the boys and a handful of specially invited guests. This was not a time to reflect upon any minor shortcomings that might still exist in Ireland's armoury, but to celebrate those all-too-rare occasions in rugby where you've achieved something quite special and are left with a memory to cherish for the rest of your life.

# CHAPTER 9

# LEADING LEINSTER

It was not long after the conclusion of the Six Nations that Brian and Glenda announced they would be going their separate ways. Their relationship had been rekindled after a previous split, but this time they both agreed that it had run its course and it was time to move on. They both led hectic lifestyles, which didn't help. Brian would be away from home for long periods with his rugby, and Glenda knew that she would not have the opportunity to spend much time with him in the upcoming summer as he would be away on Ireland's tour of New Zealand and Australia.

Meanwhile, Glenda's modelling career was going from strength to strength and she was becoming a regular fixture on Irish television. With both of them keeping busy diaries, it became increasingly difficult for them to find time to spend together.

Both parties maintained a dignified silence and there was no vicious backbiting in the press. For the time being, Brian wanted to focus solely on his rugby and, with an especially busy few months ahead with Leinster and Ireland, he needed to be completely focused on the challenges that lay ahead.

For now, his immediate priority was winning major silverware with Leinster, and, with them in contention for both the Celtic League and the Heineken Cup, he knew that his presence as a player and as captain would be vital in determining their fate. The club had come on in leaps and bounds since Michael became coach. Brian felt that his game was developing and he was improving as a player for the first time in several years. The new coaching regime had brought in a new spirit to the club, and they were seeing the fruits of their efforts on the pitch.

At the beginning of April, Brian travelled to reigning Heineken Cup holders Toulouse for a quarter-final clash. This was a chance for Brian to show off to the fans just how much the club had come on since Michael took over as coach. No player should need motivating to take on such prestigious opponents. He knew it would be a tough task overcoming the French giants, but he had faith in his own ability and felt his team were more than capable of giving them a run for their money.

Early on, a series of penalties for both sides saw Leinster leading 9–6, with Contepomi showing superb accuracy with the boot. After 25 minutes, a superb move involving Horgan and Contepomi ended with Brian bursting through the defence to score a cracking try. If the critics were in any doubt that Leinster were among Europe's best club sides, this try silenced them once and for all. At half-time, they had a 10-point lead and the three-times champions were on the ropes.

They had done everything right so far, but every player knew that a lapse of concentration or a loss of momentum could easily allow Toulouse back into the game, and there was still a tough 40 minutes to come. Sure enough, early in the second half two penalties from Elissalde and a Michalak drop goal brought the French side within a point of Leinster and suddenly they were the side in control of the game.

Just when it seemed as though Toulouse were dominating the game's possession, a loose pass from Michalak was snapped up by Cameron Jowitt for Leinster's second try. Leinster were on a roll, and more was to follow when Denis Hickie cleverly exchanged passes with Gordon and managed to squeeze over in the left corner.

Brian's men added a fourth through Horgan, and,

although Yannick Nyanga and Yannick Jauzion went over for late Toulouse tries, Leinster had done enough and Brian had led his team to one of the most famous victories in their long and proud history. This was undoubtedly the proudest moment of his club career to date, and, although he wasn't going to rest on his laurels, he took time out to celebrate this win in style and reflect upon what had been an excellent season for Leinster so far. That said, there was still a great deal of work to be done and they could still throw it all away with a few poor performances.

In mid-April, Brian was to lead Leinster out in front of a packed Lansdowne Road for a Heineken Cup semi-final against arch rivals Munster. This was the biggest game of his club career to date. Matches against Munster were always special but, with so much at stake, this game had an extra edge to it. For one, Declan was returning to his own stomping ground and Brian felt that both he and Leinster had something to prove.

And, of course, the winner would have the opportunity to face French giants Biarritz to be crowned champions of Europe. However, from very early on it became clear that this wasn't going to be Leinster's day. From the kick-off, Malcolm O'Kelly failed to gather Ronan's kick cleanly, putting the Leinster defence under immediate pressure.

After two minutes, the pressure gave and Munster

were awarded a penalty, which allowed Ronan to put his side ahead. After nine minutes, Ronan had the chance to kick for another three points but instead opted for the corner. It was an inspirational decision. Paul O'Connell took the ball cleanly from the line-out before passing to Leamy who drove through the Leinster defence to score. Ronan converted to give the away side a comfortable 10–0 lead.

Leinster finally managed to break out of their own half after 12 minutes when Hickie went on a superb break but Shaun Payne's tackle was just about enough to force him into touch. They finally got their first points on the board after 20 minutes when a nervous Contepomi kicked a penalty over. However, within eight minutes Ronan had kicked over two more penalties to make it 16–3.

Contepomi had been responsible for conceding one of the penalties and his nightmare continued in the 30th minute when he missed a penalty that couldn't have been easier. The first half had been a disaster, and at half-time Brian had some harsh words for his men to try to kick them into gear for the second half. This was a huge deficit, but one that could be overcome.

The beginning of the second half was scrappy with neither side able to control the game convincingly. Contepomi saw a well-taken 40-metre kick come back off the post, but, as time wore on, Munster enjoyed the lion's share of possession and Leinster didn't look like getting back into the game. Contepomi eventually added three points in the 68th minute but, in truth, the comeback never looked like coming to fruition.

The fighting spirit that had seen Leinster progress to this stage of the competition had gone. Ronan was able to add another try unopposed three minutes from time, and deep into injury time Trevor Halstead added another after strolling all the way from his own half to put the ball between the posts.

The final score was a humiliating 30–6 defeat. After the game, Michael put on a brave face before the camera and refused to blame Contepomi for his errors during the match. He was quick to point out that at the start of the year nobody had given him the time of day and now he was suddenly regarded as one of the world's best kickers.

Brian, meanwhile, was devastated by the defeat. He knew this was an opportunity lost. This was his best chance to date to win some major silverware at club level, and his side had blown it, and as captain he had to take his share of the responsibility. What's more, they would have booked their place in the final by beating their arch rivals. But that wasn't all. Declan's homecoming was meant to demonstrate that things had changed for the better at the club since he left. As things turned out, it looked as though they were missing him badly, although Brian believed that the decision to appoint Michael had been the right one and he was still far happier with the structure at the club as it was now.

With Leinster out of the Heineken Cup, Brian began to wonder how long it would be before he won some major silverware as a player. He was now of an age where he would have, at most, another five years playing rugby at his absolute peak, and there was now a very real possibility that he would be remembered not as a great player, but as a captain of his club, country and the Lions who showed so much promise but ultimately failed to deliver the goods.

For this reason, the Celtic League gained extra importance for the rest of the season. At the start, he felt that, naturally enough, his duties as Ireland captain would be his absolute priority. Second would come Leinster's progress in the Heineken Cup, with the Celtic League coming a very distant third. Indeed, he was expecting to be rested for a large number of Celtic League fixtures. After the Munster defeat, winning the Celtic League suddenly meant a great deal.

On the final day of the season, the Leinster squad travelled to Edinburgh knowing that they stood an excellent chance of winning the league. They had to beat their Scottish hosts, and hope that the Ospreys managed to beat Ulster, the team currently sitting top of the league.

Brian had kept one eye on this fixture since the Munster defeat and didn't underestimate the importance of this game to his career as a whole. Yes, ultimately their fate was out of their own hands and depended greatly on the Ospreys giving them a helping hand, but it was absolutely pivotal that they won this game.

Leinster started badly, and soon found themselves a man down when Will Green was sin-binned and Ander Monro had kicked a penalty over for the hosts.

Brian remembered all too well how he had felt in that game against Munster a few weeks before, and how his side had blown it very early on. He was determined not to let that happen again, and led by example to put things right. He found himself in the right place at the right time to receive a perfectly weighted feed from Horgan. There was no way he was going to mess this up and scored a perfect try. Minutes later, he scored a second when he outwitted the Edinburgh defence by finding an extra yard of pace to dart between the posts when they were expecting him to send the ball wide. This was Brian O'Driscoll at his absolute best.

With his side in firm control of the game, he almost added a third try shortly afterwards when he raced after Contepomi's grubber kick, but Edinburgh fly-half Phil Godman reached it a split-second ahead of him. Four minutes before the break, Edinburgh managed a consolation try through the veteran lock Scott Murray.

Leinster were still 14–8 up going into the break, and during the interval Michael and Brian reminded the players of exactly how bad they felt after the defeat to Munster, and how important it was not to blow this opportunity to pick up some silverware. News came through from Swansea that Ulster had a three-point lead over the Ospreys. The players didn't dwell on this fact, knowing full well that a few well-placed kicks from Gavin Henson could deny Ulster the title in the second half.

Brian remained completely focused on the 40 minutes of rugby in hand. For him, this was right up there with the most important games of his career. Get this right, and he could be parading the Celtic League trophy around Dublin on an open-top bus. This was not a time for him, or the team, to lose concentration or momentum.

Brian the two-try scorer became Brian the provider as he set up Shane Horgan, who finished it off in style. Contepomi was keen to repay Michael's faith in him, and on this occasion he didn't disappoint, bagging a typically opportunist effort late on. He added a further penalty for good measure, to give Leinster a 31–8 victory. They had done their bit, and bagged a precious bonus point along the way. Things couldn't have gone better. Now all they needed to do was to hope the Ospreys could do them a favour in Swansea.

At the Liberty Stadium, a late Jason Spice try, which an in-form Henson converted, had given the Ospreys a slender 17–16 lead. It looked like the title was going Leinster's way. Then, in the final minute, disaster struck when David Humphreys attempted a drop goal that cannoned off one post, then the other, before going over. It was one of those fifty-fifty kicks that could so easily have gone the other way, and the title would have gone to Leinster, but it wasn't to be, and the man who had captained Ireland in Brian's absence had led Ulster to the league title in the most breathtaking of games.

This was a heartbreaking way to end what had been a perfect night to date, and the whole team were shell-shocked with what had happened hundreds of miles away in South Wales. The defeat was especially hard on Eric Miller, who was retiring after 11 years' service with Leinster. For Brian, this was a difficult pill to swallow. Everything had gone right for Leinster that night, and he had played out of his skin to make sure Leinster bagged maximum points from the game. Yet events elsewhere, combined with a bit of good fortune for his Ireland colleague David Humphreys, had denied him his chance to pick up some major silverware.

It was the end of another long, hard season that had promised so much yet failed to deliver when it really counted. Yes, Brian was obviously pleased with the Triple Crown win, and he could be proud of his country's Six Nations displays after a shaky start. And, at last, Leinster were starting to look like serious competitors for the big prizes. Over the course of the season, they had beaten French giants Toulouse and had even seen off league champions Ulster in the final club game to be played at Lansdowne Road.

Yet, at the same time, they had not shown up against Munster in the semi-final. They had given up early in the second half, when there was still plenty to play for. What if they had shown some of the same spirit that had seen them destroy Toulouse at home? Things could have been very different. Again, in the Celtic League, on the big occasion against Edinburgh they had won in style, but league titles are not won and lost on a single night, and there had been some poor performances against sides they should have beaten comfortably.

At times in the season, Leinster had been breathtaking and Brian had put in some of the best performances of his career, and had captained with distinction. Things were undoubtedly heading in the right direction at the club, but they lacked consistency at key times, and occasionally looked beaten in games when there was plenty of time left to claw results back. These were things Michael was going to have to look at over the summer.

For a few days, the disappointment of the last day of the season really hurt, but it wasn't long before Brian realised that there was little more he could have done in that final game. Truthfully, they had blown it long before they went on to the field in Edinburgh and their fate was out of their own hands. It was now time to enjoy the end-of-season drinks and to give Eric a good send-off after serving the club with distinction over the last decade. Eric was only 30, but had decided that a series of injuries had taken their toll and the demands of the professional game were too much for him now. He would go on to find employment at his old school, Wesley College in Dublin, where he was to become a popular rugby coach for the under-16s and senior school team.

Brian's attentions quickly turned to the tough summer's rugby that lay ahead with Ireland. Very soon, he would be joining up with the Ireland squad and they would be flying out to New Zealand to play two Tests against the All Blacks before flying on to Australia for a further Test there.

This tour meant so much to Brian for a number of reasons. Firstly, it would be an opportunity to lay some ghosts to rest from the previous summer's Lions tour. The incident that ended his tour was gone but not forgotten, and he felt he owed it to himself to show the New Zealand public how good he was.

It was also a chance for the Ireland squad to experience playing in New Zealand and Australia, and to consolidate their excellent performances in the latter part of the Six Nations. The World Cup was a little over a year away, and Brian knew that, if his men could perform as they did in those latter games, they would be in with a serious chance of winning the tournament. This tour would give them the opportunity to pit their wits against two of the strongest sides in the world, and would also provide them with ample opportunity to make amends for the poor performances they displayed against these two rugby-proud nations in Brian's absence the previous autumn.

Eddie already had one eye on the World Cup, and he was keen to establish who his best 15 players were at this stage, to give them plenty of time to prepare, train and play together before the tournament began.

Brian left the comforts of his new home in Dublin and boarded the plane for the long flight to New Zealand believing that Ireland had what it took to beat the All Blacks. By now, Graham Henry's men were more confident than ever and believed themselves to be invincible. Brian was keen to cut them down to size, and getting one over on Henry was enough of a motivation in itself to beat the All Blacks.

This time, though, Brian would not be coming face to face with Tana, who had retired from international rugby in January. He had cited family reasons for his decision, but he was still serving a six-month ban for that tackle and was still regarded as a villain everywhere apart from New Zealand. Brian would, however, be coming face to face with Keven Mealamu once more. Keven's role in the tackle had largely been forgotten by the world's media, who tended to blame Tana entirely, but Brian regarded Keven as equally responsible. With no real apology ever coming from him, Brian felt more motivated than usual to hit him where it hurt – by making sure he was on the losing side.

Brian led Ireland on to the pitch in Hamilton for the first Test fired up and raring to go. His preparation for this series couldn't have been better. He felt in the peak of physical fitness, and his shoulder was in as good a condition as it had been in a long while. He faced the haka in the same way he had during the Lions tour, remembering the instructions the Maori warrior had given him the previous year. Then, once more, it was time for battle to commence.

However, the game plan went out of the window from the kick-off. Brian knew all about bad starts to tours in New Zealand. Fortunately, this time he wasn't to sustain a serious injury but what followed seemed as though all his weeks of preparation for this game had been for nothing.

Full-back Mils Muliaina surged through a flimsy tackle from Ronan, and handed the ball on to Aaron Mauger. The inside-centre sprinted deep into Irish territory before passing to the lightning Doug Howlett, who held off Andrew Trimble's dive to score in the corner. Luke McAlister missed the subsequent conversion, but the game could hardly have got off to a worse start for Brian's men.

He wasn't going to be beaten this early, and the humiliating setback only seemed to make him more focused and determined to defeat the opposition, and it wouldn't be too long before he got the opportunity to strike back in style. After 11 minutes, Gordon picked up a quick ball from the scrum, before passing to Brian who cut inside Joe Rokocoko and Ma'a Nonu to score under the posts.

At last, Brian had shown the New Zealand public what he could do, and caught two of the world's greatest players off-guard to put his country in front. There was no way Ronan was going to miss such an easy conversion, not on a night like this. A few minutes later, he added a penalty to make it 10–5 to the visitors.

New Zealand added a penalty of their own 10 minutes later, but some superb Irish defending frustrated them as the lead was maintained. Soon Ronan added another three points when debutant All Black loose-head Clarke Dermody conceded a needless penalty. He added another penalty with the last kick of the half, giving his country a comfortable 16–8 advantage at half-time.

Brian knew that the hosts were almost certain to come out rejuvenated in the second half, and did not underestimate the importance of keeping concentration in the early exchanges. There was no way they could allow themselves to go to sleep the way they had done at the start of the game.

Despite Brian knowing what was required, other members of the team failed to keep focused and the second half began with a blunder similar to the first. McAlister's initial dent saw Rokocoko, Nonu and Mauger combine before Muliaina finished the move. The conversion reduced Ireland's lead to just a point, and all of a sudden the reasonably solid lead they took into half-time looked very slender indeed.

Ireland regained composure, and a good period of attacking possession ended with Ronan lobbing a superb overhead pass at Trimble who touched down in the left corner. Ronan took his time and added a superb conversion, extending his side's lead to eight points once more. Shortly before the hour mark, two McAlister penalties reduced the lead to two points, and five minutes later Ronan's aim let him down as a chance to gain another three points went begging.

With nine minutes left, McAlister added another penalty to give his side the lead. Brian's men shared his desire to fight to the death, and it wasn't long before Paul O'Connell went on the attack. Incredibly, his pass was intercepted by Muliaina. He surged upfield, passed to Nonu, who continued the run and dismissed an attempted tackle from Stringer, before passing to Flavell who finished the manoeuvre in style. The conversion was added, giving the hosts a 34–23 victory.

There was no hiding Brian's disappointment in this defeat. He had prepared so well for this game and had played out of his skin, continuing the fine form he had shown with Leinster towards the end of the season. It was one bad mistake from Paul that had cost them the game, although it would have been crass to place all the blame on him. He had been having a superb game until that moment of bad judgement at the death.

After a day's pondering, Brian soon realised that there were many positive things that had come from this match. His country had just given the All Blacks a far tougher game than any of the Lions Tests had been. They had a far smaller pool of players to choose from, yet they played as a well-oiled unit for most of the game, and had it not been for a loss of concentration at vital times the result may well have been different.

He also realised just how hurt the players felt after the defeat. This meant that they were not out there for fun, and that they were deadly serious about going out there and beating a team that most commentators agreed were the world's strongest. If they had gone out there playing for pride, or were expecting to lose before the whistle blew for kick-off, they would have been far less down at the end of the game.

It was clear to Brian that they had come on a huge amount in a relatively short space of time. The abysmal displays of the previous autumn now felt like a lifetime ago. This was a side that, with a year's solid preparation, stood a very real chance of winning the World Cup. As for this tour, with one more match to come against the All Blacks, there was everything to play for.

This time around, Brian had even less time to soak up the culture and atmosphere of New Zealand. The second Test was only a week away and once that was over they would be flying straight on to Australia. Yet the gloom that had dominated his mind for much of the Lions tour didn't occur this time. He was feeling far less homesick and felt far happier about being away from home. There could have been a number of reasons why this was the case.

Maybe being single allowed him not to have such an emotional tie to home and allowed him to concentrate on his rugby. The fact he was actually a part of the playing squad also helped. He did not feel like a spare part lying around looking for something to do all the time, which is how he ended up spending the majority of the Lions tour. This time, he was a playing captain who was working with Eddie and the boys on every aspect of the preparation for the big games. He had a purpose, and this made being away from home all the more bearable.

He had also changed his psychological preparations for the big games. He was no longer as obsessive about the game that lay ahead. Well prepared, certainly, but he did not 'close down' in the way he had done in the week leading up to the first Lions Test. He had remembered how unfair it had been to shut Glenda and his family out the way he did, and this time he was far more jovial to be around while he was on tour.

Having a long injury lay-off had taught him that, while winning games and tournaments was massively important, he had to learn to enjoy being a professional rugby player more. He knew that there were millions of people all over the world who would happily swap jobs with him, and it dawned on him that he was, after all, doing the one thing he had always wanted to do since he was a young child, and he had to learn to enjoy seeing the world and playing the game he loved on the big stage.

The following week, Brian finally got the chance to lead his side out at Eden Park, Auckland in the second Test. The referee was Brian's old friend Jonathan Kaplan, and he went out there as determined to win as he had been the previous week. In the intervening days, Eddie had been working with them to iron out the silly errors that had cost them victory last time around and Brian was keen to make sure they gave their absolute best.

Ireland found themselves up against it from the start as the All Blacks controlled early possession, but Ronan fell marginally short with an early long-range penalty. But the hosts were in control and Byron Kelleher burrowed over after Geordan Murphy had lost possession.

New Zealand remained in control and, midway through the first half, Chris Jack drove for the line and appeared to play the ball while on the ground, but referee Kaplan waved play on and Clarke Dermody dived in for the score. McAlister added a penalty before Brian's men struck back in style.

Paul O'Connell broke free of a weak covering tackle to charge over under the posts, with Ronan adding a further two easy points. Soon after, Ireland had the All Blacks trapped on their own line. They earned a series of penalties, but they opted for the line-out instead, so confident were they that this aspect of their game had finally been sorted out.

From the second line-out, Ireland drove for the line and Flannery was awarded a try. Ronan converted, bringing the scores to 20–14 at the break. One more converted try and Ireland would be in front.

In the second half came a traditional New Zealand downpour. Ireland's new resolve was going to be tested and they would have to succeed in difficult conditions if they were to take anything from this game.

Brian led by example and was pivotal in keeping Ireland in the game early in the half. After 10 minutes, a penalty from Ronan reduced the deficit to just three points. The rain continued to fall heavily, making the ball greasy and the surface slippery, with both sides struggling to control possession.

With eight minutes remaining, McAlister took the ball 10 metres out, crashed straight through Ronan O'Gara's challenge and touched down under the posts. He converted his own score to increase the lead to 10 points. The game was lost, but, in truth, it was far closer than the score suggested.

This time, however, Brian had few complaints. Ireland had given it their all in tough conditions, and there were no glaring errors that cost them the game. In the post-match interviews, he was full of praise for his team's spirit and resilience, saying that if one break had gone their way the result might have been different.

As the tour prepared to move on to Australia, Brian could find no major faults in his game or with his team's progress. Some of the rugby played in the two Tests wasn't pretty, but the conditions weren't easy and, in the second Test in particular, if they had been a tad more lucky the result would have been different, and Ireland would have smashed a century-old winless record against the All Blacks.

The squad touched down in Australia genuinely believing they had what it took to defeat what had been an indifferent side over the past year. On paper, the sides looked fairly evenly matched, although the Australian team were more established and one would naturally expect home advantage to count in their favour. Both had seen their share of ups and downs over the past year and both had put in some pretty half-hearted performances in the previous 12 months.

Brian was keen to display just how much he and his team had moved on since their last meeting at Lansdowne Road the previous autumn. He led his team out on to the field in Perth determined to show their class. It had been a good week in training, and they had consolidated all the good work they had put in over the previous two games. What could possibly go wrong?

The home side had the better of the early exchanges and went ahead through a Stirling Mortlock penalty on 14 minutes. They extended their lead midway through the half when Chris Latham scored to make it 8–0. Ronan and Mortlock exchanged penalties, leaving Australia with a comfortable lead at the break. Brian was furious with the half-hearted display his team had shown in the first half. This 40 minutes of rugby was a major step backwards for the side, but the lead was not large enough for the game to be dead and buried and Brian called on his men to put on a fighting display in the second half to show the Australian crowd what the new Ireland were made of.

With Brian's words ringing in their ears, they made a far better start to the second half. Early on, Ronan's high cross-kick was caught by Shane Horgan, who fed David Wallace and his pass was well taken back by Ronan for a fine try on 47 minutes.

They struck again just three minutes later when Neil Best scored in the corner following some good work from Andrew Trimble and Denis Leamy. Ronan kicked over the conversion to put the side 15–11 in front. This was more like the play Brian expected from the team.

As quickly as the team came into form, they lost it again. Their lead lasted only five minutes, when Australian winger Mark Gerrard broke through for a clinical first-phase try. After this, Ireland went to pieces and the Wallabies added no fewer than three further tries in the closing stages. Firstly, loose-head Greg Holmes pounced on a loose ball before running half the length of the field to touch down. Further scores followed from George Gregan and Cameron Shepherd to condemn Ireland to a 37–15 defeat.

After the game, Brian cited fatigue as the main reason for his side's poor performance, especially in the final 30 minutes. He told reporters that three weeks of tough Test matches had taken their toll, and that the legs had started to get heavy. He also said that the series had taught him that, while Ireland had made considerable progress, there was still a very long way to go and there was major work to be done if they were to be serious contenders for the World Cup.

Despite the obvious disappointment Brian was feeling, he felt he could not have done much more to win the game. After all, he had been playing in tough, physical contests since the start of the year and there had been very little time to allow his body to rest and recuperate in the last six months. He knew that another tough season with Leinster was little over a month away, and that the next set of internationals were only a few months down the line.

Brian decided that, when he got back to Dublin, it would be time to take it easy for a few weeks before the next battles began. The demands on a modern professional rugby player may be high, but he knew full well that nobody could play that standard of rugby all year round without it having some kind of an impact, and that resting was actually a very important part of preparations. The next few weeks would be about taking it easy, catching up with the family and having a few good nights out with the boys.

As soon as he got back to Dublin, it was time to let his hair down and party. Being single, and on a night out with your mates, has its dangers as Brian was about to find out to his cost in what was one of the most embarrassing things that had ever happened to him.

On a night out, he got talking to a girl and they swapped phone numbers at the end of the night. Unbeknown to Brian, one of his friends had got hold of his mobile and replaced her number with his, while keeping her name. The following day, 'she' sent Brian a very interesting text and he replied in kind. The messages were quickly getting more and more spicy and Brian became quite excited. Once his friend had finished having fun, he told Brian the truth, which he later described as one of the biggest disappointments of his life.

It wasn't long before he was back in training and preparing for the long, hard season that lay ahead. As things stood, Brian would publicly say that Ireland were in with an outside chance of winning the World Cup, but he now knew who he'd be facing in the Pool stages; clashes against France and Argentina were going to be tough games in their own right and there was no point in looking beyond them at this stage.

The Ireland squad met up in early November to prepare for three autumn internationals against South Africa, New Zealand and the Pacific Islanders. It was time to test the new Irish resolve against Southern Hemisphere opposition on home soil. As an added incentive, these games were to be the last international rugby matches to be played at Lansdowne Road before it closed for redevelopment, and every player wanted to send the old place off in style.

First up came that game against South Africa, which turned out to be a classic, and one that will long be remembered in the hearts of every Irish rugby fan for all the right reasons. South Africa took first blood through an Andrew Pretorius penalty but conceded the opening try after just four minutes.

Ireland were on the attack and won a scrum 10 metres out which they used to bring Trimble in from the left wing, allowing the powerful Ulsterman to charge through to score. Ronan missed the tough conversion, but soon made up for it by adding a penalty to make it 10–3.

The in-form Trimble began the move that led to Ireland's second try in the 25th minute by breaking through several tackles before recycling. Quick hands and sharp thinking saw the ball moved right where Ireland had numbers and Horgan drew his man before supplying the scoring pass to Wallace who raced in under the posts. A surge from Marcus Horan at close range saw Ireland lead by an incredible 22–3 margin at half-time.

The Irish defence was made to work hard early in the second half, but held up well after several periods of intense pressure. South Africa finally managed to score their first try after 65 minutes when new cap Francois Steyn dived over in the left corner. Bryan Habana soon added another after the ball was swept over to the right. Brian was beginning to fear the worst, and knew that this was no time to be losing concentration.

He rallied his troops and they reacted well by hitting back immediately, when Brian's back-handed pass set up a historic try for Horgan. The conversion was soon kicked over by Ronan, making the final score Ireland 32 South Africa 15. This was one of the most famous days in Irish rugby history and Brian had been the man who captained his team to glory against one of the world's best teams, playing one of his best ever games for Ireland in the process.

In the post-match interview, there was no hiding Brian's delight when he declared that Ireland could now beat any team in the world. Eddie was slightly more modest with his reactions, pointing out that South Africa had fielded several inexperienced players. But even he was delighted with the performance his boys had put in and he finally began to see several years of hard work with this group of players coming to fruition.

Naturally, Brian and the boys enjoyed a few beers in Dublin that night, but they could not afford to celebrate for too long as they were just days away from another big game against Australia.

The tired, lethargic Ireland team that had been soundly defeated by Australia just a few months before had been replaced by a confident, attacking, well-oiled machine that was more than capable of defeating any side that was not completely on top of its game. Brian knew this was an opportunity not to be missed.

The Lansdowne Road crowd knew that Ireland weren't just there to play for pride or make up the numbers. Every Irish rugby fan knew that, if their team won, they would have proven that the previous week's win was not just a fluke and they would be right up there with the giants of world rugby.

However, it was Australia who took first blood when skipper Stirling Mortlock kicked over a penalty after just four minutes. Not long after, Ireland thought they had scored in the corner through Murphy but the television replay showed that the Leicester full-back had not quite got the touchdown. Instead, play was taken back and Ronan kicked over a penalty which went through after first hitting the post.

Ireland enjoyed the better of the opening exchanges and controlled possession well, and they finally got the try they had been threatening for some time on 25 minutes when Ronan spotted Hickie on the left touchline and kicked cross-field. The Leinster winger caught the ball cleanly before outmanoeuvring three defenders to score an excellent try.

A minute before half-time, Ireland added a second when some superb handling from Ronan released Gordon, who rushed forward before feeding Shane Horgan, who in turn managed to pass to Geordan before he was pushed into touch. Geordan managed to finish an excellent move to put Ireland 15–3 up at the break.

It had been a classic 40 minutes of rugby from the home side and they received a well-deserved standing ovation from the 43,000-strong crowd as they returned to the dressing room.

The second half lacked the pace and drama of the first half but in the early stages Australia added another penalty score. However, Ronan hit back with two more in quick succession for Ireland.

At one stage it was 14 men against 13 as Denis Leamy along with Aussie pair Mat Rogers and Phil Waugh were sin-binned for fighting. Hickie came close to getting another try but Ireland had already done enough and Australia never looked like getting the extra points to snatch the game, leaving Ireland with a 21–6 victory – only their second victory over Australia in 27 years.

Brian had not got his name on the scoresheet, but his judgement and preparation as captain had been superb and he thoroughly deserved the vast praise he received after the game. At last, everything Brian had thought possible over the past few years had come to fruition. Brian had never doubted that this Irish squad had what it took to perform on the big stage and be right up there with the world's best, and now, at long last, they were beating the giants of world rugby on a regular basis.

Yet neither Brian nor Eddie became complacent. Both knew that there was a danger that, with the winter break from international rugby, the squad could easily take a major step backwards and all the old errors and scrappy play could return for the Six Nations campaign in February.

Another concern facing Eddie and Brian was that the squad might lack the depth required to win the following year's World Cup. Certainly, the first-choice XV had proven they were a match for any team, but, as injuries inevitably took their toll over the course of a long tournament, would they have the depth in the squad to succeed?

Eddie took the decision to make no fewer than nine changes for the final match of the autumn against the Pacific Islanders. He saw it as important to keep Brian in the squad because, as captain, he would have to work with these players. One of the changes saw Paddy Wallace coming in for Ronan at fly-half.

This was also to be the final time Ireland would play at Lansdowne Road before the old place was demolished and rebuilt. Brian shared the view of the majority of Irish fans that this redevelopment was necessary to give Irish rugby a world-class arena on the scale of the Millennium Stadium or modern-day Twickenham, although there was no denying this would be a day of mixed emotions. Yes, Lansdowne Road looked dated and the facilities and size of the ground was not as good as many others around the world, but there could be few places guaranteed to generate such a noisy, passionate atmosphere anywhere in the world and for that reason it would be greatly missed.

Ireland started the game confidently when a clever reverse pass from Wallace sent Hickie through for the first try after five minutes. Wallace added a conversion and a penalty came soon after that gave the home side some early confidence.

But the visitors struck back after 12 minutes thanks to a converted try from Seru Rabeni. Wallace added two more penalties to give Ireland a nine-point cushion but this really did look like a side with nine changes and Ireland were lacking rhythm and the class they had shown in their previous two matches.

With mistakes creeping in, the Islanders added their second try on 34 minutes when Lome Fa'atau scored after a turnover. Shortly before half-time, Ireland managed two tries in quick succession through Wallace and O'Kelly, who scored after impressively stealing the ball from the line-out.

At half-time, it was clear that Girvan Dempsey was feeling the effects of a strong first-half tackle from Rabeni and was replaced by Gordon. Ireland then started the second half much more brightly and they managed to score another two tries in quick succession. Brian set up the first one when his off-load sent Easterby through, while Horgan bounced off a tackle to race to the line. Both tries were converted by Wallace, who was proving he was more than capable of filling Ronan's boots if called upon.

Brian went off injured after 58 minutes with what appeared to be a recurrence of his hamstring injury, although his removal from the game was really little more than a precautionary measure.

He watched from the stand as Ireland added further tries through Easterby, Rory Best and O'Connell, but Wallace spoiled his excellent form early on by fluffing the final two conversions. But he had already done enough to win the man-of-the-match award, in a match Ireland won 61–17. The win may not have been as classy as in the previous two games, but the new boys had done well in their first game together and it was a fitting send-off for the oldest rugby ground in the world.

After the game, a contented Brian reflected on the achievements over the last three matches, which reinforced his belief that this side was now the greatest in the Northern Hemisphere at least. He had been generally impressed with what he had seen from the second-string players and was confident that they would gel as a team if they were given sufficient time to train together.

He was, however, slightly frustrated that the squad now had to break up until mid-January when they had been in such full flow. Of course, there was nothing he could really do about that, and the reality was that he and everybody else had club commitments in the few months that lay ahead.

Brian broke with his usual routine of heading off for a few beers at the end of a series. Instead, he headed straight to a local hospital to visit his sister and new niece who had been born two days earlier.

There was hard work ahead, but right now life couldn't be better for Brian.

# CHAPTER 10

# A DATE WITH DESTINY

The year that would define Brian's career had almost arrived. Everything looked perfectly placed to put him at the centre (in more ways than one) of the greatest year Irish rugby had ever seen. By now, Brian was considered by many pundits to be the greatest centre in the world, and, among Irish fans, as one of the best of all time. 2007 could prove to be the year that sealed Brian's place in history.

On paper, things couldn't be better. Although things hadn't quite materialised with results on the pitch at Leinster, Brian was more than happy with the progress the side were making since Michael took over as coach. With Ireland, things really couldn't have been better after the autumn they had just experienced, although Brian and Eddie were both wary of the trap of complacency.

For the time being, though, Brian needed to focus on his club duties. Leinster had made an indifferent start to the season in Brian's absence, having suffered three defeats and one draw in their opening nine Magners League fixtures. Over Christmas, Brian took to the field at Thomond Park, Limerick, for the traditional derby against Munster.

Matches against the old enemy still meant as much to Brian as they ever did and he still absolutely hated losing to them. He took to the field determined to give his best and to lead his men by example. However, they would have to do without the services of the excellent Contepomi, who was out injured, which allowed Jonathan Sexton to make his Magners League debut.

The new boy made an impact within five minutes when he kicked a penalty over but Munster soon responded with a period of concerted pressure that led to them being awarded a penalty try following a collapsed scrum after 13 minutes, which was soon converted by Ronan.

Leinster responded in style with Girvan Dempsey scoring in the corner just five minutes later. Ronan soon put another penalty over to give Munster a 10–8 lead but it would be Brian's men who would have the upper hand at the break, when Munster flanker

Frankie Sheahan was sin-binned for a professional foul in added time and Sexton converted the subsequent penalty.

Only three minutes after the break, Ronan added a penalty for Munster, and added a further two within a short space of time, while Sexton pushed a long-range effort wide. As the second half progressed, the home side reinforced their dominance as their forwards pressurised Leinster who became increasingly prone to mistakes.

Despite bringing on a half-fit Contepomi late in the game, he was not able to make much of an impact and Munster won the game 25–11.

Although Brian always hated losing to Munster, this defeat hurt more than most. He had failed to get into the game and penetrate the Munster defence, and the rest of the team had not managed to get into gear and confront a well-oiled Munster unit. However, he had been impressed with Sexton's debut and knew he would have plenty to offer the side at some stage in the future. A few days later, Leinster managed to go some way towards making amends for the defeat when they beat Ulster at home, 20–12, ending 2006 on a high.

In mid-January, Brian met up with the rest of the Ireland squad at the City West hotel in Dublin to begin preparations for the upcoming Six Nations campaign. From the outset, Eddie and Brian both knew exactly what they expected from this campaign, and that was to achieve the Grand Slam. After all, there was no reason why they shouldn't.

The three autumn internationals had been a huge success, but the reality was that in a few years' time nobody outside Ireland would remember just how good they had been in those games. For this team to be remembered throughout the world, they had to pick up a major trophy. Brian believed his task was to beat every major nation in the Northern Hemisphere, achieve the Grand Slam and hold up the Six Nations trophy in March. For this side, anything else would be a disappointment.

Yes, they had achieved the Triple Crown this time last year, playing some breathtaking rugby in the latter stages of the tournament, but Brian knew that the side had come on a great deal since then. He also knew that other nations had upped their game in the intervening 10 months.

England could well return to form with the recent appointment of the experienced Brian Ashton as coach. Scottish rugby was still on a high after the previous year's success, while Italy would inevitably continue to improve, as they had done every year since joining the tournament. France, meanwhile, were rarely poor for any more than the odd game here and there and were always likely to prove tough opposition.

In the weeks leading up to the first game, Eddie focused the training on making sure they were as well drilled as they had been in the autumn, and were ready for the long campaign that lay ahead. The build-up to the tournament couldn't have gone better. Brian was confident that the preparation had once again been spot on and they would continue their run of fine form.

The first match was away to an out-of-sorts Wales side that was still feeling the ramifications of the debacle that erupted during the previous year's tournament. However, Brian knew their new coach Gareth Jenkins well from the Lions tour and had a great deal of respect for what he had done with the squad in New Zealand, and also admired what he had achieved with the Llanelli Scarlets side. As Simon Easterby would be quick to point out, Gareth was a passionate man and no team he coached would lack commitment, and therefore they could not take this game for granted.

Brian led his team out at the Millennium Stadium for their first match in front of 74,000 noisy fans. This was it; the start of the year when Brian would show the world what he and the Irish team were made of.

Things couldn't have got off to a much better start when, after just 46 seconds, Brian blocked Stephen Jones's kick, allowing Rory Best to gather the loose ball and flop over the line. Ronan missed the subsequent conversion, but the breathtaking start had left the Welsh crowd shell-shocked.

Wales soon fought back into the game and made some

good ground, which resulted in a penalty opportunity for Jones, which he kicked over the bar with ease.

The pace of the game was electrifying and the crowd produced deafening volumes of noise, with both sides playing exciting, attacking rugby in the opening 20 minutes. Ronan missed a difficult penalty kick and then had to watch Jones kick one of his own over to give the hosts a 6–5 lead.

A period of fierce Welsh pressure followed, which eventually resulted in Jones kicking over another penalty, while Hickie spilled blood and had to go off for stitches. This left Geordan replacing him temporarily on the left wing.

However, Ireland soon fought back and Wallace skilfully burst through several Welsh tackles before passing to Brian, who scored his 17th Championship try in the right corner. Ronan kicked the conversion that followed, and Ireland were back in business thanks largely to Brian's sharp judgement. They had a 12–9 lead at half-time.

Ireland nearly lost the lead shortly after the break when Chris Czekaj broke clear down the left, sent a grubber past Andrew Trimble and seemed destined to gather and score. But Simon Easterby clipped the Blues wing just enough to slow him, the infringement going unpunished, allowing Ireland full-back Girvan Dempsey to get back and slap the ball away.

## A Date with Destiny

In the 64th minute, James Hook had a kick charged down by Ronan that led to him claiming a third Ireland try. Gordon made the decisive break, brushing through Czekaj too easily to get to within inches of the Welsh line and Ronan was on hand to dive over despite Hook's despairing tackle.

With the game almost certainly won, Ireland felt things had gone more or less to plan on the day. However, disaster struck five minutes from the end when Brian hobbled off with a recurrence of his dreaded hamstring injury and was now a real doubt for the upcoming big clash against France.

This was a real worry for Eddie and the boys and they all felt nervous about losing their captain and star player for what was likely to be a Championship-deciding game. For the whole squad, this twist of fate took the gloss off what had been a well-earned victory.

As the week progressed, it became clear that Brian wouldn't be able to lead his side out against France. This was a double blow for him. Obviously, he had wanted to play in the big game. Matches against France suited his style of play and he always gave his absolute best for these games. They meant a huge amount to him and being injured came as a bitter blow.

Secondly, this was Ireland's first match at Croke Park, where they would be playing their home matches while Lansdowne Road was being redeveloped. There were massive historical and political connotations associated with this occasion and Brian had been looking forward to leading his team out in front of an 82,000-strong crowd since the announcement had been made to play the matches there.

Paul O'Connell was to captain Ireland in Brian's absence. Brian was sure this was the right decision and had every confidence in his ability to lead the team on this big occasion.

Brian took his seat in the stand for the game, knowing full well the significance of this game. The hairs stood up on the back of his neck as he soaked up the unique atmosphere of Croke Park. He had long been a fan of Gaelic sports and had visited the stadium many times before, but to have Irish rugby internationals being played in this huge arena meant a great deal to him. He was desperately sorry he wouldn't be leading the boys out himself, but he had to put those thoughts to the back of his mind and think of the team as they prepared for battle.

The match was every bit as physical and demanding of the players as Brian had expected it to be. Just three minutes in, O'Connell was penalised for killing the ball, allowing David Skrela to kick France into a three-point lead. Six minutes later, the fly-half added another three points from in front of the posts when Rory Best was adjudged to have interfered at a ruck.

Ronan got a penalty back for Ireland in the 14th minute but it was becoming clear that they were going to be up against it for the rest of the game. French captain Raphael Ibanez soon broke through a weak tackle from Geordan, and ploughed passed the challenges of Marcus Horan and John Hayes to cross the Irish line.

However, Ireland fought back in style and Ronan soon added another penalty. They kept the momentum going and on 32 minutes Ronan scored a try in the corner following an impressive run of play involving Hickie, Horgan and Wallace. However, the kick was at a difficult angle and he failed to add a further two points. Skrela missed with two penalty attempts before half-time, leaving his side with a two-point advantage at the interval.

Early in the second half, Geordan sprinted towards the line after France lost possession but referee Steve Walsh had already blown his whistle for a knock-on without playing advantage. Despite this setback, Ireland seemed to be controlling the game and Ronan kicked his side into the lead for the first time on 56 minutes.

The game continued at a frantic pace and was a fitting curtain-raiser for life at Croke Park. Replacement Lionel Beauxis hit the post with a long-range drop goal attempt which would have put France ahead again.

Ireland looked to have won the game when Ronan added another penalty to give the side a four-point lead with two minutes remaining, but right at the end of play Vincent Clerc ran through the Irish defence for a French try, with Beauxis converting to make the final score 20–17 to France. The crowd, who had been so vocal throughout the game, sat in stunned silence. Ireland hadn't been at their brilliant best but they had controlled the game for much of the second half and the game looked in the bag right up until the last play of the game. In truth, the team were probably missing Brian's influence as captain and, had he been on the field, the result may well have been very different. The confrontational style of the game would've suited him perfectly and there was no hiding his disappointment at being forced to sit helplessly in the stand as his team crashed to a last-minute defeat.

The defeat was a bitter pill to swallow, but Brian knew that another massive game against England was just a fortnight away and he began looking forward immediately. He was highly likely to be back fit for the game and preparations had to begin now if they were to defeat a rejuvenated England side.

Eddie and Brian made sure that all the boys were looking forward, rather than backwards. The Grand Slam was gone but there was still every possibility of their winning the Championship, and the Triple Crown was still very much on. In training, they focused on sorting out their defensive line, which had been a substantial weakness in the game against France, while Brian spent the first week of the fortnight gap doing some gentle exercise. He didn't want to overwork the hamstring as he knew from past experience how fragile it was, but by the end of the first week it was clear he was fit and able to lead the boys out against England.

At last, Brian's chance to take to the field at Croke Park had arrived. Once again, the place was buzzing and the crowd expected nothing but the best from Ireland now that Brian was back and in top shape. He got the physio to give his hamstring a rub shortly before kick-off. He knew there was a chance that, if his hamstring got cold during the anthems and presentation to the dignitaries, it could give way early in the match. Spending so long out in the cold standing still before the game wasn't ideal preparation for him, but decorum and tradition dictated it had to be done.

It was England who struck first through a Jonny Wilkinson penalty, but Ronan replied in kind soon afterwards. The opening quarter of the match was fairly even but two further penalties from Ronan saw the Irish leading 9–3 after 26 minutes. Both sides struggled as a massive downpour fell on Croke Park making conditions difficult with a boggy ground and slippery ball. However, it was Ireland who adapted best to the conditions and after 30 minutes came a moment that would swing the match firmly in their favour.

England just about managed to stop the rampaging Simon Easterby but Danny Grewcock cynically went offside at the ruck and was yellow-carded. From the resulting penalty, Ronan kicked the ball into the corner. The visitors managed to hold back the initial driving maul, but, after a poor pass from Stringer, some quality passing from Gordon and Brian rescued the manoeuvre, before passing to Dempsey who touched down in style, with Ronan adding the extras.

Shane Horgan nearly added another but a last-ditch tackle from Mathew Tait denied him, though Ireland remained firmly in control of the game. A period of sustained pressure resulted in a try from Wallace after 38 minutes, with an on-form Ronan adding the conversion to give Ireland a 23–3 lead at the interval.

The game looked firmly in the bag, although Eddie and Brian were quick to remind the team that complacency had cost them dear before and they could not afford to lose concentration for a moment as the game could still be snatched from them as it had been against France.

Ronan stretched the lead further with a penalty shortly after the break, but England hit back in style when the debutant David Strettle slid over in the corner. Jonny added the conversion and a penalty followed soon after. Ronan restored Ireland's 16-point advantage when he struck back with a penalty of his own after

Julian White was punished for illegal use of the boot in the ruck.

From then on, it was Ireland all the way as they launched a series of threatening attacks on the England line, which were in no small part down to Brian's efforts. His best attempt nearly saw him cross the line but he was narrowly held up by Mike Tindall. From the resulting scrum, Ronan cross-kicked and Horgan towered above Josh Lewsey to claim a superbly executed try.

In the dying moments of the game, replacement scrum-half Boss claimed a late interception try to finish off what had been a superb display by Ireland, giving them a 43–13 victory. This was England's heaviest ever defeat in the history of the Championship. The Croke Park crowd gave Brian's men a standing ovation as they left the field.

This was the Ireland side that had looked like world-beaters the previous autumn, and this match proved just what an important part Brian played in the team. It was as though his presence could turn a talented but disorganised group of players into one of the most disciplined and focused rugby teams in the modern era. Right now, though, Brian's priority was capturing the Triple Crown which was very much still on.

Next up came Scotland, a side that had blown hot and cold during the Championship so far. They went crashing to an away defeat to England in the first week, but had gone on to thrash Wales at home a week later, before being on the receiving end of a 37–17 drubbing by Italy in the previous round of fixtures. Eddie and Brian both knew that this Scotland team were capable of providing tough opposition, but they were terribly inconsistent, a bit like the Ireland team of 18 months previously. They realised that in the intervening fortnight they had to prepare thoroughly and remain disciplined and well drilled as a team.

Brian arrived at Murrayfield knowing that this was a golden opportunity to retain the Triple Crown. To win it once was impressive, but to win it two years in a row, and three times in four years, showed the squad had true class. They may have blown the Grand Slam for another year, but the Triple Crown was no easy feat and a win here would see the current Ireland squad go down in the record books as one of the Championship's all-time great sides.

Brian led his warriors on to the field, backed by a massive Irish contingent who had made their way across the sea for a weekend in Edinburgh, hoping to paint Prince's Street green that night. Ronan kicked a penalty over to give Ireland the lead after seven minutes, but, despite some powerful Irish surges, Paterson scored the first try of the match for Scotland just eight minutes later, the circumstances of which will not be remembered as Brian O'Driscoll's finest hour.

## A Date with Destiny

The Scotland skipper was caught by Hickie while on a run and, when he was on the floor, Peter Stringer caught him in the head. A minor brawl ensued, and Brian was very lucky to get away with a warning from the referee when the situation had calmed down. Ireland had seen many examples of fine team leadership from Brian in recent times, but this wasn't one of them.

Ireland hit back when a Dan Parks kick was charged down by Ronan, who passed to Gordon, who exchanged passes with Easterby, before passing back to Ronan who touched down. In truth, it was a soft try caused by some sloppy Scottish defending of the sort that had caused them to be thrashed by Italy two weeks earlier, but Ireland were back in the game and, for Brian, that was all that mattered. Paterson added two penalties and Ronan added another before the half-time break, which Ireland went into leading 13–9.

Brian made up for his silly antics early in the second half when he sprang two great breaks, but the rest of the team failed to give him the support he deserved to make the most of it, most notably when Shane Horgan was guilty of a poor forward pass when a try looked certain.

Scotland fought back and scored another penalty to reduce the deficit to just one point. Suddenly, Ireland had to be on their guard. On the hour, Paterson kicked over another penalty to give the home side the lead. However, the hosts were just as jittery as Ireland had

231

been and Ronan hit back with a penalty of his own to give Ireland a 19–18 victory, with him scoring all of Ireland's points.

That was it – another Triple Crown in the bag. It wasn't Ireland at their most fluid and eloquent, but rugby isn't always pretty and Brian was more than aware that sometimes you just had to knuckle down, get stuck in and grind out results, and this was just one of those occasions. However, celebrations were muted following a nasty incident that could have left the hero of the hour, Ronan, seriously injured.

In the closing seconds of the game, Ronan found himself at the bottom of a ruck that somehow left him choked. According to Eddie, someone had their arm around his neck, cutting off his air supply, and he went blue. The doctor came on and soon made sure he was all right, but that could have been a very serious incident. After looking at the replay, the independent commissioner found no blame with any Scottish player and nobody was punished.

Going into the final day, no fewer than four teams could theoretically win the Championship. Ireland's task was to beat Italy in Rome in the first game of the day and hope Scotland did them a favour against France.

Brian led his team out on to the pitch at the Stadio Flaminio not underestimating the size of the task ahead. Italy had just been through their best ever Six Nations

Championship, and they were now a team that did the basics very well and were more than capable of beating any of the traditional five nations on their day. The Ireland team had prepared seriously in the week leading up to the game, knowing they might not be able to afford the sort of errors that had crept in during the match against Scotland.

After Ronan put Ireland in front through a penalty, Pez equalised with a drop goal before putting another penalty over soon after. Any ideas the Irish fans had about this being an easy game to win were soon dispelled.

However, this Ireland team were back on top form and their first try of the afternoon came after Gordon and Brian had done some good build-up work to allow Dempsey to score in the left corner with 16 minutes played. Five minutes later, Horgan sent Easterby wide to score Ireland's second. Italy needed to hit back fast, and the superb Pez soon added another penalty and drop goal to cut Ireland's lead to just one point. Ireland scored a controversial try to end the half when Hickie's scoring pass to Gordon was clearly forward but he was allowed to play on and score Ireland's third.

After the break, Ireland were keen to remind the world of the sort of rugby they had been playing the previous autumn, and managed to put through four tries in 13 minutes. Dempsey charged through a large gap over the line, with Ronan adding the conversion. The floodgates had opened when Hickie danced through Italy's midfield before passing to Horgan who finished off in style. Hickie crossed himself following a crafty dummy and then O'Gara was over, chasing a kick after D'Arcy had broken from his own half.

With Ireland seemingly unstoppable, Brian's Championship came to an unfortunate end when the dreaded hamstring gave way once again completely out of the blue, and he had to be helped to hobble off the field. He was obviously disappointed that his game was to end early, but he had captained his team with distinction and there was no way they could lose it from here.

Marco Bortolami got Italy's first try on 74 minutes but Ireland replied with Hickie's second of the game. A stoppage-time touchdown from Roland De Marigny in the corner made the final score 51–24 to Ireland, but little did they know that the late consolation try for Italy would cost them the Championship just a few hours later.

The Ireland team returned to the hotel to watch France take on Scotland in Paris, knowing that the title was on a knife-edge. The first half was very close, with Scotland at their best, forcing France to push very hard, but in the second half the difference in power began to tell and the home side scored a few tries to stretch their lead. After 80 minutes, they were three points behind Ireland, so they pushed forward.

## A Date with Destiny

A try was awarded to Elvis Vermeulen following a decision by an Irish Television Match Official, which was highly controversial because it could barely be seen on the replays. The match referee asked him if there was any reason why he thought the try shouldn't be awarded, implying that he had already decided that it should be given.

This close call had deprived Ireland of the Championship in the most cruel way imaginable. It had been the most dramatic and nail-biting conclusion to a Six Nations Championship ever, and, as with all tense sporting dramas, one side was left on the receiving end of a painful and bitter defeat. Brian and the boys were stunned into silence. As the clock ticked down in Paris, it looked as though they had done enough. Indeed, many of the players could justifiably think they had the Championship in the bag. Few would argue that Elvis Vermeulen had been on the receiving end of a very fortunate refereeing decision.

It turned out that, for the thousands of Irish fans watching the France match on big screens and in cafes, bars and restaurants in Rome, there had been an extra cruelty for them to endure.

Because the match had over-run its allocated time slot, French television had cut the feed to other countries, meaning that a large number of Irish fans lost pictures from Paris a few moments before the end, and had naturally assumed Ireland had done enough and began celebrating. It was some time before news filtered through of what had actually happened right at the end of the game.

This had been one of those 'what if' occasions. What if Ronan had landed his goals? What if Brian hadn't been forced to go off injured? What if Andrea Scanavacca had missed his conversion? What if Paterson had landed his? Brian's men had come so near, and yet the atmosphere at the end of the game in Rome somehow implied that Ireland hadn't quite done enough.

To make matters worse, Brian's injury was more serious than he had first feared and Eddie was worried he might be facing a lengthy lay-off. Despite this, Eddie made it known in the interviews that followed that he would not be allowing his squad to dwell on this painful setback for too long because the opportunity to grab a far bigger prize was only a few months away.

It wasn't long before Brian's mood was lifted when he discovered he had been named RBS Player of the Tournament for the second year running following a fans' poll on the official tournament website, with over 10,000 votes cast for him. This was a testament to the high esteem in which he was now held not just in Ireland, but also by rugby fans the world over. Despite Ireland falling short of expectations, few now doubted that Brian was one of the best centres, if not the very best, in the world.

## A Date with Destiny

Meanwhile, with the press unable to talk about Brian's rugby performances, they soon turned their attentions to the latest goings-on in his private life. The press were speculating that he was dating actress Amy Huberman, probably best known for her role in RTE's *The Clinic*. As with previous relationships, Brian was keen to keep things as low profile as possible. They both had careers of their own and it soon became clear that neither of them wanted to be part of some sort of celebrity golden couple. However, they had now been together for several months and a certain amount of press attention was inevitable.

It soon became clear that Brian wouldn't be returning to club duty with Leinster for the remainder of the season. The priority now was getting him fit for the World Cup in the autumn and there was no point in risking him in these comparatively minor games.

The club, meanwhile, were experiencing a disappointing climax to the season. After being thrashed by Wasps in the quarter-final of the Heineken Cup, their only hope of winning any silverware came on the final day of the season when a win away at Cardiff would give them the Magners League title.

Brian travelled to Cardiff to give his men moral support for this vital game. As with the previous season, the league had gone down to the final week of fixtures. Leinster entered the match knowing that a win plus a bonus point for scoring at least four tries would secure the title, regardless of whether the Ospreys managed to win their final game.

However, after just six minutes, Nick Robinson made the crucial break, accelerating past a surprised Keith Gleeson before swinging a superb pass to Robin Sowden-Taylor to score a textbook try as he sucked past Denis Hickie.

Felipe Contepomi, who earlier in the day heard he had qualified as a doctor, got Leinster on the scoreboard with a brace of penalties, bracketing one from Blair for the home side. Both sides struggled to cope with the pitch, which had become sticky after several days of heavy rain in the Welsh capital. It therefore came as no surprise that the next try was a forward effort for the home side finished off by hooker Gareth Williams, giving the Blues a 13–6 lead at half-time.

Michael knew at half-time that Leinster were in danger of throwing it away at the last minute once again, and that a massive effort in difficult conditions was needed in the second half. Unfortunately, they were unable to click into gear and the Blues added two further tries in quick succession. The first was engineered by Nick Robinson whose fine cross-kick was fielded by Chris Czekaj on the right to send full-back Rhys Williams over, with Nick Robinson converting.

Not long after, Marc Stcherbina benefited from a

crucial error when Horgan muffed a chip, allowing him to gather the ball and take it over the line. Horgan managed to make amends on 55 minutes when his grubber was mis-fielded by Rhys Williams, allowing the Ireland back to hack on and touch down. Contepomi missed the subsequent conversion and then found himself sin-binned for out-jumping Jamie Robinson in mid-air. This game was turning into a disaster for Leinster exactly when they didn't need it.

Hickie and Gordon continued to make decent breaks but they lacked support and there were handling errors at key times, condemning Leinster to a 27–11 defeat. The title was lost to the Ospreys, who got the win they needed at Netherdale the following day. Although he was not on the pitch that day, there was no hiding Brian's disappointment at coming so close, yet being pipped at the post once again, for the umpteenth time in his career. The lesson of the season for both club and country had been that, while both sides were packed with talented players, Brian's presence on the pitch, both as a player and leader, added an extra dimension to the side that turned them from losers into world-beaters.

In his personal life, in June, Brian attended the wedding of Ireland's fitness coach Michael McGurn. For once, he and Amy made little effort to hide from the waiting press as they posed for photographs, complete with trendy sunglasses, outside the church in

Enniskillen. This was taken as a clear sign by the press that this was now a long-term relationship and that things seemed to be going well.

With the domestic season over, attention soon turned to Ireland's preparations for the biggest tournament of Brian's career to date – the Rugby World Cup 2007.

# CHAPTER 11

# THROWING IT ALL AWAY

One thing that had become clear over the last six months was that, while Ireland's strongest XV were capable of beating any side in the world, there were real concerns that the squad lacked the strength in depth required to win the World Cup.

It was inevitable that, during the long World Cup campaign, injuries would occur to key members of the squad and backup in all positions was needed. With Brian out injured, and Eddie concerned about key players becoming injured at this crucial time, he decided to take a largely second-string squad for the two-match tour of Australia.

The results were clearly not Eddie's main objective,

241

but getting squad cohesion and injecting some competition to avoid complacency from the first-choice XV were right at the top of his priority list. Yet, even so, the performances were disappointing. In the first game, Ireland crashed to a 22–20 defeat thanks largely to Contepomi's superb kicking, and in the second they lost by an embarrassing 16–0 scoreline. This was hardly the message they wanted to be sending to Argentina, who they would be facing for real in the group stages of the World Cup.

In early August, the squad met up at the City West hotel to begin preparations for the World Cup. This was it – the time had arrived when this squad, who had proven they could beat any side in the world, set out to prove they really were the best rugby team on the planet. The early signs were encouraging. Brian had recovered from his hamstring injury and was now at the peak of his physical fitness. There were no major long-term injury concerns in the squad and there was no obvious reason why this side wouldn't win the tournament, or at least come very close.

Their first of two warm-up games would come away at Scotland in mid-August. Eddie knew the time for experimenting was over and his first-choice men needed a chance to get match-fit. Brian led his men on to the field expecting nothing less than a convincing win. Scotland had gone backwards in the last year and, while spectacular at times, had not had as good a Six Nations campaign as they would have hoped. A victory here was the minimum requirement.

However, it took just three minutes for Ali Hogg to break through the Irish defence to give the home side the lead, with Paterson adding the conversion. Paddy Wallace cut the gap for Ireland but the Scots were in full control and it came as little surprise when they added a second soon after when Andrew Henderson muscled his way over for his sixth international try, which Paterson duly converted once again to make it 14–3. This looked like a very different Ireland side to the one that took the world by storm the previous autumn and the alarm bells started ringing for Eddie and the fans.

Geordan added a penalty but Ireland just never looked like getting into the game and were guilty of making silly errors, and shortly before half-time Scotland added a third try when Ewan Murray crossed the line to make it 19–6 at the break. Needless to say, Eddie made his views abundantly clear in the dressing room.

With Eddie's scathing words ringing in their ears, the boys came out for the second half determined to put things right. The game was still winnable and there was no reason why, with discipline and concentration, they could not still grab a victory from this mess.

Yet it was Scotland who struck first with Henderson's second try of the game. But after this they began to become complacent and Ireland started to work their way back into the game. Tommy Bowe's break led to the ball reaching Isaac Boss who evaded both Lamont brothers – Sean and Rory – to score his team's first try of the afternoon and spark Ireland into life. Trimble added another in the 55th minute before Wallace added a penalty to make it 24–21 at the midway point in the second half. Ireland had got stuck in and fought their way back into the game. This was more like it from Brian's men, but, once again, concentration seemed to slip and this allowed Scotland to creep back in and score one more try through the superb Henderson, to give Scotland victory by 10 points.

Brian had come off in the second half with a tight hamstring and sore wrist but this was little more than a precautionary measure. However, there was no ignoring the fact that Ireland had once again slumped to a defeat when he wasn't on the pitch and it may not have been entirely coincidental that they lost concentration at around the time he was replaced. However, the main injury concern that arose from the game was Shane Horgan, who twisted his knee and was now a serious doubt for the World Cup. Shane had been instrumental in Ireland's successes over the last few years and Brian feared, with some justification, that losing a player of his calibre for the World Cup would leave Ireland a significantly weaker team.

As the evening progressed, it became clear that Shane would be out of action for roughly four weeks. When the squad was officially announced the next day, his name was included, meaning he was in with a chance of making the second Pool game against Georgia. The main omissions from the squad were Trevor Horgan, Mick O'Driscoll, Keith Gleeson and Jamie Heaslip, while Eddie decided to choose Brian Carney, who had only converted from rugby league a few months earlier, over Tommy Bowe.

At midweek, the squad travelled to France for a match against Bayonne that Ireland won 42–6. Brian had recovered from his hamstring injury and captained the side to a comfortable victory. However, a nasty incident took place during the game that threatened to jeopardise Brian's participation in the World Cup. What should have been a minor warm-up game had turned into a game Irish rugby fans would long remember for all the wrong reasons.

During the second half, he was punched by lock Mikaera Tewhata as he approached him to break up a row, in what was a blatant act of violence that brought back memories of the Tana incident on the Lions tour two years earlier. The impact of the punch fractured Brian's sinus. He required nine stitches just below his right eye, and the doctors warned him that there was a danger of infection due to there being pockets of air in his battered eye socket. There were even fears for Brian's sight in that eye, let alone whether he'd be able to play rugby again. This was not what the Ireland squad needed so close to the World Cup. Once again, Brian had been on the receiving end of an unsporting act that would threaten to rule him out of what should have been one of the highlights of his career.

With just one more game to go before the World Cup started, it was important Ireland put in a strong performance in their final warm-up game against Italy, which was the first international to be played at Ravenhill in Belfast in half a century. The ground played host to many Ireland matches until 1954, when it was abandoned for internationals in favour of Lansdowne Road. Yes, they would have to do without Brian, Shane Horgan and David Wallace, but this needed to be the game where they proved that there was depth in the squad and they could cope without Brian, as it seemed likely they would have to do without him for the first few games at least.

The 14,000 full house watching should have witnessed a try in the third minute after Denis Leamy's break but Denis Hickie opted to go it alone instead of passing to Girvan Dempsey and was bottled up by the Italian defence.

Ronan managed to kick the first Irish penalty after six minutes, but, instead of building up momentum, they started to lose their way somewhat. In the 21st minute,

Ronan's loose clearance was gathered by the Italian full-back David Bortolussi, who took the opportunity to kick a superb drop goal from 10 metres out. Shortly afterwards, a brawl broke out between a number of players after Sergio Parisse had thrown a punch at Peter Stringer.

Ireland regained composure and Stringer gathered Ronan's superbly placed kick to score a try. Ronan added a conversion but Bortolussi added a penalty to narrow the gap to just four points. In the closing minutes of the first half, the strong Italian scrum exerted pressure and Ireland finally lost the lead when a tap-penalty saw Alessandro Troncon charge through for a try, with the video referee giving the correct decision in Italy's favour. Bortolussi added the conversion to give his side a 13–10 lead at the interval.

Geordan was prominent as Ireland made a rousing start to the second half, and Ronan eventually kicked a penalty over after an earlier attempt just moments earlier had hit the woodwork. However, Ireland's attempts to break down Italy's robust defence came to nothing. Trimble's break in the 72nd minute after an Italian fumble set up a chance for Hickie but the Irish wing didn't have the legs to get past Kaine Robertson. However, Ronan restored Ireland's lead in the 74th minute with a superbly taken long-range drop goal. In injury time, Matteo Pratichetti notched a breakaway try after Peter Stringer had fumbled the ball in the Italian half. Geordan claimed the try-scorer had impeded him in the build-up but the try was awarded and the conversion duly followed.

Ireland looked beaten. But deep into injury time Trimble's forward-looking pass sent Ronan charging towards the line. There looked to be major doubt over whether Ronan had grounded the ball after being challenged by Kaine Robertson but the score was awarded, much to the relief of the Ravenhill crowd, giving Ireland a 23–20 victory.

After the game, Eddie told reporters that he was disappointed with the team's stop-start performance, but praised their character in getting back into the game. However, this wasn't good enough for much of the Irish public, who were rightly furious as they had witnessed an embarrassing display that was disjointed and lacked rhythm. This certainly didn't look like a side that was going to beat the world's greatest teams within a few weeks and Eddie's statement that they were not 100 miles away from clicking didn't go down well with many people.

The game had highlighted once again the importance to the team of having Brian on the field. As had been the case before, without his leadership and commitment they soon fell to pieces and wouldn't threaten an average Six Nations team, let alone the world's best.

To the astonishment of many, within days of the

embarrassing victory the IRFU announced an extension to Eddie's contract that would see him remain in charge until 2012. This decision was criticised by many within the Irish media, who saw this as taking much-needed pressure off him to deliver a strong performance at the World Cup.

Meanwhile, as the days passed by, it became more and more likely that Brian would be able to play in all of Ireland's Pool matches. However, the squad remained tight-lipped on his progress. After all, what would be the point in letting their rivals know that he would be OK when they could surprise them with his inclusion in the squad and ruin their game plan in the process?

By the end of August, Brian had regained 80 per cent of his vision in his right eye and he was expected to fully regain his sight in time. He was also back in training and his stitches would be out within days. Brian couldn't hide his delight at the astonishing progress he had made and was getting himself into shape for the most important tournament of his career.

Brian boarded the plane with the rest of the squad as they flew to France in early September. But it wasn't long after landing that the problems that were to haunt the squad for the duration of the tournament began to come to light. They were taken by coach to a hotel in a dreary part of Bordeaux. At first sight, many of the players couldn't believe how little research the IRFU had put into choosing the hotel. This was not the sort of place Brian or any other professional rugby star was used to. Yes, there was a video room and a 'private sport room', but the facilities just weren't up to scratch and there was very little to do in the surrounding areas. This did not compare to the sort of places Brian was staying in during the Lions tour of New Zealand. This stark 1970s concrete block did not feel like the sort of place Brian would want to spend a month living in.

More bad news was to follow when the camp was rocked by reports in the French media that Ronan had racked up gambling debts of more than £250,000 and that he had separated from his wife Jess. Ronan angrily denied the accusations, describing them as 'despicable' and reassured his team-mates that, while he clearly enjoyed gambling on horses, he had not been an excessive gambler and was fully in control. He was furious with the suggestions that he had been kicked out of his home and made it clear that they were still very much in love.

As for the rugby itself, there was no denying the scale of the challenge that lay ahead. The media had dubbed the Pool 'The Group of Death', with Ireland having to face Argentina and France in the weeks ahead, with other, supposedly easy matches against Georgia and Namibia to play as well. Indeed, it would be Namibia who would be Ireland's first opponents. Brian had by now made an excellent recovery and was named in the starting line-up. The circumstances were far from perfect and the preparation had been terrible in so many ways, but Brian remained keen to prove that his was still one of the best sides in the world and his ambition of leading his country to World Cup victory remained very much alive.

Brian led his men on to the field in front of 32,000 fans at Stade Chaban-Delmas in Bordeaux expecting nothing other than a clear, convincing victory against one of the tournament's supposedly lesser sides. It didn't take long for Brian to make a statement of intent when after just four minutes he scored a try, running on to his own chipped kick and shrugging off Ryan Witbooi to make himself Ireland's sole leading try-scorer of all time. Ronan then added the conversion and a penalty followed soon after.

Ronan was clearly keen to silence those who had made such hurtful comments in the press, and set up Ireland's next try on 29 minutes by taking a tap penalty and kicking to the right corner where Trimble gathered before touching down. On the stroke of half-time, Namibia fly-half Emile Wessels landed a long-range penalty.

Early in the second half, the referee rightly awarded Ireland a penalty try following two collapsed scrums, and Namibia could have few complaints, securing the Irish a bonus point in the process. Yet, in the final quarter, Ireland fell to pieces and Namibia managed to play some decent rugby, and in the 61st minute big blindside forward Jacques Nieuwenhuis thundered over for a try. Another soon followed when Piet van Zyl touched down. However, Ireland scored one more when Flannery was a tad fortunate to be credited with a try in the left corner, and Ireland had a 32–17 victory.

Yes, they had won, but they had been truly awful on occasions. That said, Brian led by example and seemed to be the only player on the pitch worthy of wearing the green shirt for much of the game. His commitment levels were exemplary from start to finish. If the reports of complacency within the squad were to be believed, Brian would be the name right at the bottom of the list of players on the field that night who were taking their selection for granted.

Following the game, Brian didn't mince his words, describing it as a really awful display that started badly and got worse as the game went on. There were no excuses. It was a victory, but it really felt like a defeat. There was a huge amount of work to be done before the next game.

Just six days later, Ireland returned to the Stade Chaban-Delmas for what should have been a straightforward game against Georgia. Brian had shrugged off a minor elbow injury sustained in the match against Namibia and it was clear both he and the squad had to give their absolute best in this game to look like serious competitors for the tournament. After all, it was less than a year since this group of players had been beating some of the world's greatest sides. Where had it all gone wrong? Surely they still had it in them to do it – there was no logical reason why they shouldn't be able to.

Ireland took the lead after 16 minutes when the pack grabbed a line-out and drove through the Georgian forwards, before Ulster hooker Best got over the line. Ronan added a difficult conversion. Ireland failed to improve on this try and for much of the first half there were elementary mistakes, with only Brian threatening the Georgian defence, but he couldn't do it all by himself and his team-mates let him down throughout the rest of the first half. Late on in the half, a powerful charge from George Shkinini swept Georgia out of their own half and, when openside David Wallace had been sin-binned for killing the ball, Merab Kvirikashvili stepped up to slot the three points.

The stadium was stunned shortly after the break when Georgia took the lead. Peter Stringer sent a looping pass in Brian's direction but it was intercepted by Shkinini. The Blois winger galloped home under the posts with Kvirikashvili landing the conversion. This was turning into a humiliating and shameful performance. However imperfect their preparations had been, there was no excuse for struggling against such lowly opposition.

It took 10 minutes for Ireland to work their way back into the game when Gordon ran through midfield before passing to Dempsey who managed to score. Panic over, but this did not disguise the fact this was turning out to be one of the worst performances in Irish rugby history, and even now a Georgian fight-back wasn't out of the question.

Georgia dominated for long periods in the second half, and the stadium was on tenterhooks when Denis Leamy denied Georgia late on, with referee Wayne Barnes seeking confirmation from the video referee that the ball had been held up. Ireland had won the game 14–10, but this was another truly awful display, and they risked being thrashed by the more renowned opposition in the two games that remained.

Georgia had given a good performance, but Ireland should have played far, far better. After the game, both Brian and Eddie were incredibly upbeat considering the unconvincing nature of the win. Ever the gentleman, Brian praised the Georgian performance but he knew that Ireland would now have to win their matches against France and Argentina to progress beyond the Pool stage. Eddie, meanwhile, told the press that there were a lot of positives they could take out of the game and that Georgia played really well. This angered many rugby writers and supporters back home. There was no doubt that many players had been fed up with staying at the hotel and preparations in training had not been ideal, but, even so, the exact reasons why the side had declined so much so quickly remain a mystery. What was clear was that Brian was the only player on the pitch who looked truly world class and dedicated during the tournament so far.

As the week progressed, it emerged that Geordan seemed to be inexplicably out of favour. This was the man who, a few years previously, had been described by the Irish media as the 'George Best of rugby' and was now felt by many to be the man who could turn Ireland's fortunes around, and end their dependence on Brian to turn on the class against quality opposition. Thus far, his only appearance in the tournament had been as an 80th-minute replacement against Namibia.

When Eddie named his squad to play France, Geordan's name was completely omitted, with his place on the bench being taken by Gavin Duffy. Eddie's team selection had not gone down well with Irish fans. Whatever the ins and outs of what went on, this was not the kind of pressure they needed with their crunch match against France just a few days away.

As they failed to secure a bonus point against Georgia, they needed to beat the French to stand a realistic chance of progressing to the quarter-final stage of the tournament. Brian led his men out in front of 80,000 passionate fans knowing that this game was just as important for the host nation, who had experienced an earlier slip-up against Argentina. This was one of the most important games, if not the most important, of his career to date. He knew full well that the Irish public expected nothing less than 100 per cent from the team and there would be no excuses if they failed to deliver.

Yet it was the French, buoyed by the home crowd, who took the lead through a penalty after Ireland failed to retreat the full 10 metres following an earlier infringement. Shane Horgan was back at long last, and he soon made his presence felt, when in the 18th minute his superb tackle denied Clement Poitrenaud a certain try. However, Ireland were adjudged offside in that move and Elissalde knocked over a simple penalty. This was not a great start, but Ireland were looking far more committed than in the earlier two games.

Just four minutes later, Elissalde knocked over another penalty to extend the French lead. Ireland, meanwhile, seemed to be relying heavily on Ronan's up-and-unders, but they failed to materialise into anything approaching a try, although he did manage an impressive drop goal from 25 metres out in the 36th minute. The last act of the half saw Elissalde boot his fourth penalty of the night to make it 12–3 to the hosts.

This Ireland side was the best that had taken to the field since the Six Nations, but they still looked a long way from the team that were defeating the Southern Hemisphere giants less than a year ago. They made an encouraging start to the second half with Brian clearly showing that he did not think the game was lost yet, but after 55 minutes Elissalde added another penalty to make it 15–3. The deficit was now looking large, though not unassailable. Yet just two minutes later the French scored their first try of the match when Michalak put through a kick with the outside of his right boot to the right corner and it fell perfectly for Clerc.

Brian's men never looked like recovering from this major setback, and more was to follow when Paul O'Connell was sent to the bin. His absence seemed to deflate Ireland's spirits and France soon scored their second try when Clerc collected Elissalde's chip and forced his way over for a second score in the corner, the Television Match Official confirming the score.

What started out as an evenly matched contest had turned into a battering and Ireland didn't manage to add any further points, the final score being a 25–3 drubbing. After the game, Eddie citied lack of discipline, especially in the first half, as the main reason for the team's defeat. He was the first to admit that there could be no excuses and the better team had won. As for Brian, he had shown commitment and leadership throughout the game but had never been allowed the chance to make a game-changing contribution.

With one group game against Argentina left to play, Ireland had their work cut out. Their opponents had been playing some of the most impressive rugby of the tournament so far, and their brand of well-disciplined, flowing and exciting rugby had led many to believe that they were now serious contenders for the tournament. Few would now argue that Argentina were among the world's leading rugby teams and Ireland would have to give their absolute best to beat the South American giants.

However, Brian knew that, to progress in the tournament, a win alone would not be enough. Their failure to pile on the points against Georgia meant that his side would need to score four tries to progress to the quarter-final stage. Brian obviously knew Felipe Contepomi well from Leinster, and understood fully the mammoth task that lay ahead of him. Yet he also knew that this was an aim worth pursuing. Four years was a long time to wait for another opportunity. By the time the next World Cup came round, it was unlikely he would still be Ireland captain, and age would dictate he would be lucky if he was still playing international rugby at all. Even so, there was no way of knowing how naturally gifted the Ireland squad of four years' time would be. This huge task, although daunting, was also a once-in-a-lifetime opportunity he could not afford to miss.

The match took place at the historic Parc des Princes, which was the home of French rugby for many decades, and, sadly, also the scene of many an Ireland thrashing. It was time to make this a place for Irish rugby fans to remember for the right reasons. Geordan was back in the starting line-up, and there were no major injury worries. This was Brian's big chance to put things right.

The game started promisingly as Ireland controlled possession in the opening 10 minutes, but they failed to make the pressure count and it was Argentina that made the opening breakthrough. After a solid scrum, the ball was worked to winger Lucas Borges who ran over with the Irish defence in a muddle.

Ronan kicked a penalty to bring Ireland back into the game but Argentina replied almost immediately with a drop goal from Juan Martin Hernandez. Despite Ireland being behind, Brian was showing signs of being at his most dangerous, and eight minutes before the break he brushed aside some tame Argentinean tackling to score a memorable try. Ronan added the conversion to give Ireland the lead.

However, it was just four minutes later that Hernandez produced his second drop goal to give Argentina the lead once again. Brian, Ronan and Geordan were having superb games but the Irish defence looked shaky and this allowed Argentina to add their second try through Horacio Agulla just before the break, with Contepomi adding the conversion to give the Pumas an 18–10 lead.

Brian was not giving up yet. He had led by example by scoring that try, and, if by sheer hard work and dedication they could somehow tighten up their defence and score another three in the next 40 minutes, they would be in the quarter-finals. It was a tall order, but not an unassailable one.

Seven minutes after the break, Geordan scored a 47th-minute try after the ball was swung out to the right flank from a line-out. He was having a great game, and was showing just what a class act he was. His absence in Ireland's earlier games was now looking like an extremely poor piece of judgement on Eddie's part, and all those who had voiced astonishment at his absence from the team sheet were proved right. Nobody will ever know what impact Geordan could have made to the team if he had played in those earlier games, but it is not inconceivable that he could have turned the matches in Ireland's favour.

Ireland failed to add to the momentum and two Contepomi penalties and a third Hernandez drop goal sealed Argentina's emphatic victory, 30–15. Despite Ireland not being at their best, it was clear that Argentina were going to have a big role to play in the World Cup.

After the game, Brian was deflated, but dignified in defeat. This was the second time his side had been knocked out of the World Cup by the Pumas. He made it clear to reporters that, in his view, the blame lay squarely with the players, believing that there was only so much coaching that could be done, and ultimately it was up to the 15 men who wore the green jersey on the pitch to deliver the goods.

This was a once-in-a-lifetime opportunity lost forever, and was undoubtedly a bitter pill to swallow for him. In truth, they had probably left too much to do against one of the tournament's best and most exciting teams. They were beaten by the better side, but why were Argentina the better side? It had been less than a year since Ireland were giving master-class performances against the giants of world rugby.

Eddie made it clear that he would not be walking away from the job, but was lost for a valid explanation as to why the team had declined so much in such a short space of time. The only possible explanation from him was that the team had not had enough match practice leading up to the World Cup, yet they played no competitive matches at all in the weeks before the Six Nations, in which they played so well.

For Brian, this was just the latest bitter blow in a career that has seen more than its share of bad luck. Certainly, he is one of the best centres, if not the very best, in the world, and his place in history as one of the all-time greats is secure. He has established himself as a worthy team leader for club, country and the Lions, and has gained a hard-earned reputation as a man who leaves nothing to chance and who prepares his team thoroughly and properly, and leads by example on the pitch. Even during the World Cup, when those around him were faltering, few would dispute that Brian always gave of his absolute best.

In training, he puts himself through a punishing and highly disciplined schedule to make sure his body is in the peak of physical condition come the big games. Even in times of injury, he does not let himself go, keeping to a tightly controlled diet so that, when the time comes to get back into training, it is never too long a wait before he is in top condition.

Yet Brian's career to date seems to have been dominated by bad luck. At Leinster, he has failed to win any major trophies, with the exception of the Celtic League title in season 2001/02. It is true that the side has been unlucky in a number of tight games over the past few years, but the lack of trophies in the cabinet has undoubtedly been a matter of massive frustration for him.

He seems far happier at Leinster now and enjoys a good relationship with coach Michael Cheika. Rumours had been circulating for several years that he was planning to abandon the province and play his rugby in France. However, it now seems likely that he will remain at Leinster for the foreseeable future, and will only look to play elsewhere in the twilight of his professional career, if at all.

At Ireland, the closest he has come to picking up major honours has been the Triple Crown on three occasions.

Thus far, he has not managed to win the tournament that has eluded Ireland since 1985. As we have seen, this has been down to a combination of injury, bad luck, chance and a failure of the team to click and perform on vital occasions.

The Lions tour of 2005, which should have been the pinnacle of his career, the time where he could show the world what an outstanding leader and player he was, became a tour to remember for all the wrong reasons. In his mind, the pre-tour preparation and build-up to that first Test could not have gone better, yet his dreams were shattered by an outrageous tackle by someone who should have known better than to behave like that in the name of sport. The Lions never seemed to recover from this setback and the tour, which had been planned to perfection in minute detail, fell to pieces within no time.

What has become clear is that, for both club and country, Brian's leadership has been vital to the team's success on the field. If he is injured, or is away from his club on international duty, they often lose the hunger to win, and the teams seem to lose their focus and discipline. This shows the extent to which Brian is vital to the team's success. His presence on the field can turn a game. A few well-chosen words in the dressing room can psych up any team to give their best once they get on the pitch. His dedication and commitment to the cause seems to rub off on those around him.

If he stays relatively free of injury, he can expect to have another three to four years of being at the absolute peak of his powers as a player. His status as one of the world's greatest ever outside centres is secure, and by the time he retires it is quite conceivable that people will look back on his career and regard him as the greatest ever.

However, there is no denying that he will also be remembered as one of the unluckiest players ever to play the game. The gods have not been kind to him. Injuries have occurred at the worst possible moments, and events far beyond his control have impacted upon performances on the field. Yet there is still time to put things right.

Brian appears happy with the progress being made at Leinster and they are showing signs that, under Brian's leadership, they will be a force to be reckoned with in the Heineken Cup in the coming seasons. For Ireland, meanwhile, the IRFU's inquiry into the World Cup debacle is ongoing, yet we know from the autumn of 2006 and 2007 Six Nations campaigns that the team is capable of truly breathtaking rugby.

The chance to captain the Lions to victory in the Southern Hemisphere is probably lost forever, yet there will still be a chance for him to play a major part on the field when the Lions tour South Africa in 2009. By then, Brian will be one of the experienced old heads of the team, yet will still be young enough to perform at his absolute best. This must surely be a challenge on the horizon he is already relishing.

Brian's career so far can be summed up as being one dominated by breathtaking individual performances, superb team leadership and total dedication to the cause. Yet his rewards remain few and his trophy cabinet relatively bare. As a human being, he has shown himself to be a hard, battling competitor on the field, yet humble in victory and dignified in defeat, never slow to heap praise on worthy opponents.

To the public, he is reserved, yet approachable, a man willing to sign autographs for fans who approach him, while remaining shy of the limelight. There have been plenty of opportunities for him to enjoy the trappings of fame, yet he prefers to keep his private life private, and does not surround himself with excessive luxury or signs of wealth. Instead, he seems at his happiest when he is enjoying a few beers, or a summer barbecue in the company of good friends, while never forgetting those who have helped take him to the top.

For Brian's sake, and for the sake of the sides he represents and leads with distinction, we can only hope that the horrendous run of bad luck that has dogged his career will come to an end. All true rugby fans hope that Brian O'Driscoll's best days are still to come.